Wet Earth and Dreams

Wet Earth and Dreams

A NARRATIVE

OF GRIEF

AND RECOVERY

Jane Lazarre

Duke University Press

Durham 1998

© 1998 Duke University Press

Printed in the United States of America

on acid-free paper ∞

Frontispiece photo, text, and jacket design

by C. H. Westmoreland

Typeset in Monotype Fournier

by Tseng Information Systems, Inc.

Library of Congress Cataloging-in-

Publication Data appear on the last

printed page of this book.

Some of the names in this work
have been changed.

FOR L.

Acknowledgments

I owe special thanks to Sara Ruddick, Ruth Charney, and Douglas White, who read each chapter as it was being written and gave me courage and faith.

For their careful editorial responses, I thank Carol Ascher, Jan Clausen, and Jaime Manrique. For her help in many ways, I thank Claire Potter.

My sons, Adam Lazarre-White and Khary Lazarre-White, are two of my most trusted readers. I can never express the importance to me of their devotion and understanding of my work.

There are two readers whose support was central to my decision to publish this memoir. For their close readings and confidence in this work, I thank Nancy Barnes and Sarah Lazarre-Bloom.

Once again, I am grateful to the wonderful people at Duke University Press, especially my editor, Valerie Millholland, and Emily Young and Sarah E. Ball Damberg, for their insights, responses, and conversations.

As always, I thank my friend and agent, Wendy Weil, for her support.

My family and friends guided and strengthened me through the experience that became this memoir. I thank them all for their notes, gifts, calls, attentions — for their steady love.

— Hands dripping with wet earth

head full of shocking dreams

O what have you buried all these years

what have you dug up?

—Adrienne Rich, "Calle Visión, 9,"
Dark Fields of the Republic, Poems 1991–1995

When I awoke in the recovery room after two hours of anesthesia, during which time a cancerous tumor two centimeters large had been removed from my breast and eleven lymph nodes from under my arm, the threat which I felt I had to resist at any cost was unconsciousness. The moment I woke up, despite tubes and nausea and a horrible sense of amnesia — hours and a dramatic experience simply gone, erased, as this computer can be made to erase passages, pages, entire files — the very moment I awoke and heard my doctor's voice, then my husband Douglas's, eventually my son Khary's, I wanted to sit up, be told everything, return to the fullest possible awakeness. But I was being pulled back into sleep, and even though the nurse was my ally, wanting to bring me "out," telling me to breathe and stay awake, something menacing, I felt, was pulling me "in" or downward, a downward place where I fully believed death waited for me, or where I would lose my mind. I had no idea at the time why Khary's hand, more than anyone's, was the hand I needed, but I clung to it as if I were the child, he the parent, as if his exquisite devotion could literally save my life. I forced my eyes to remain open with all the will I possessed, and when my friend, Leona, who is a nurse, came into the room and whispered, "Try to stay awake, get up and walk, you have to pee before they will let us go, and we have to get the fuck out of here," I felt I was in good hands. My surgery was "outpatient," meaning I was intended to go home the same day, and although I was aware that this new system existed largely to increase the profits of insurance companies, and due to many delays all day it was nearly midnight, I was determined to get home as fast as I could.

And so, after an hour of vomiting, talking, peeing, and

walking, Leona pushing me from behind so the nurse on duty wouldn't notice, I was finally in a taxi heading uptown to my apartment.

I woke up several times in the middle of that first night with a sense of joy, the ecstatic feeling of power that comes with escape. I was alive. I was awake. I had spoken to Adam, my son who lives in Los Angeles; I had held Khary's hand. I could get up and walk to the bathroom alone. I was heavily bandaged, a drainage tube was attached to my side, and I was feeling strange pains up and down my right arm, but I was in my own room. The window was open and the breeze cool. No strangers were in sight. Lying next to Douglas, intent upon remaining awake as long as possible, I could go over and over the past twelve hours in my mind, trying to recapture as much of my lost reality as I could.

I relived my arrival at the hospital the previous day where, dressed only in a thin hospital gown, crowded into a room with strangers similarly clad, we all waited for surgery together, yet each alone, our loved ones banished for some reason to a far-off waiting room. After three hours, I began to grow anxious and begged the nurse to check on when I could expect my turn to finally come. She flipped on a computer and an operating room appeared on the screen. On the bed in the room, a woman lay on her side in a state of what appeared to be semiconsciousness: her legs crossed vulnerably, her gown barely covering her back and buttocks, which were turned to the camera. Quickly, the nurse switched off the screen and said, "You see, we're waiting for a place to move her so you can go in, but the recovery room is still full."

Another hour would pass before my doctor came to fetch me and we walked, like two girlfriends out for a date, both of us in hospital greens and large paper slippers, down the hall, into the elevator, down another hall, and into the brightly lit operating room where I was instructed to climb onto the table and an anesthesiologist inserted a tube into my arm. The last thing I heard was my doctor's voice saying, "So, David tells me you have written lots of books. What are their titles?" David has been my doctor for twenty-five years and is also a friend who has taken an authentic interest in my work. But even in the increasing haze, I realized this was just a form of being asked to count backward from ten to one, and so, instead of answering her, I said, ten, nine, eight, and then I lost time.

I was only vaguely aware of a disturbing familiarity at the very center of my happiness as I lay in my bed, staring at the walls, the curtains, the shadows of my quilt on the ceiling as I moved my knees. I was afraid of sleep, which had for years been a balm for me. If it weren't that I felt so relieved and even joyous, I'd have been reminded of my childhood when chronic insomnia made every night a nightmare long before any dreams began.

The Self That Self Restrains

In the spring of 1995, the condition I seem to have been waiting for all my life finally struck me. I was trying to keep afloat after three difficult years full of crises and disappointments. I knew I had to move to a new stage or phase of things, to unencumber myself of old, tiresomely repeated themes, and especially to liberate myself from the anxieties and fears of disaster that stalked my days, as they had off and on for more than a decade. I thought I could face whatever network of defenses and distortions had held these fears in place so long, but I was losing the battle for a sense of control and becoming increasingly depressed. A surprising characteristic of the depression was my ability to go on functioning in the world at a level of ordinary competence so that only my very best friends, or those who were for some reason interested in being especially observant of me, noticed. I taught my classes, mentored my students, remained extremely involved with the lives of my grown sons, and was even engrossed in the writing of a book about the dramatic changes in my perspective on myself and my society as a result of living for more than twenty-five years in an African American family, the white Jewish mother of Black sons. Yet there is no question that I was seriously depressed, if that overused word continues to suggest a sense of unalleviated, bleak hopelessness, chronic physical fatigue, sadness with seemingly no end, loss of sexual desire, and, at times, the wish to die.

I felt like two women: the one everyone knew—teacher, writer, mother, provider, attentive wife and friend; and *that other one*, as I began to call her. The girl/woman who above all was constantly afraid, at least some part of every day subject to visions of disaster destroying me or those I loved, especially Adam and Khary, my sons.

I'd be away on vacation with a close friend, and as I walked home from a lovely day at the beach, a "vision" would come to me that local police were waiting to tell me my family had met with a terrible accident and were all dead. I could see the faces of the police, careful and worried; I could hear their solicitous voices; I could picture myself packing, rushing home to identify the bodies. My heart would begin racing as we neared the little cottage where we lived for a week or two in idyllic peace and remote beauty. Whatever conversation I was having with my friend would fade into the background as I struggled to argue against myself, trying to dismantle the ineluctable reality of my sudden fear. And I could not relax into normality again until I had made a call home, ascertained that all was as I'd left it, not suddenly, irretrievably lost.

Or, lying in bed in the middle of the night waiting for one of my sons to come home (if they were visiting, or home for vacations during their college years, or living at home for a time while in a transition between college and the next stage of life), I'd be attacked (it felt like an attack from the outside which instantly permeated the deepest recesses of my inner self) by the conviction that they were hurt, either by gun-wielding cops or sociopathic young muggers, and I'd have to get up and pace the apartment, drink water, sweating and crying, sometimes for hours, until I heard the key in the door.

Over the years I tried to convince Douglas of how much I needed reassurance rather than anger during these bouts of hysteria. But anger—because I could spark his own anxieties and because nothing disturbs him so much as people being out of control—was always close to the surface of his reactions. And it was not until that spring of 1995, when I got breast cancer, and its six-month aftermath of painful and frightening treatments, that he came to believe in my inability to control my panic at times, despite honest and strenuous attempts to do so.

Whenever I was subject to these bouts of fear, and they came more or less often depending on many factors, it felt as if all order, design, and predictability were gone from the world and everything in it. Chaos reigned, an evil chaos, like a curse or supernatural punishment, incomprehensible to ordinary consciousness yet making some terrible sense. An explosion might occur suddenly, blowing my or some loved one's body to fragments of unidentifiable tissue and bone. A car filled with drive-by shooters might murder one of us for no reason, any time, any place. A subway could be derailed and all its passengers killed. Any and all natural and man-made disasters seemed not only possible, which the nightly assault of local and national news broadcasts assured me they were, but imminent. Even the character of my children could fall into a chaotic world where nothing was known or reliable. They are both stable, strong young men, neither of them at all self-destructive. Yet, I could suddenly have a fear of one of them committing suicide, tortured by some torment or despair utterly hidden from me.

When I look back now, feeling stronger each day and having been given a very good prognosis, though always frightened of the recurrence of cancer, I understand that my life is changed forever by the diagnosis, the lumpectomy and removal of lymph nodes that permanently changed the feelings and capacities of my right arm, by six weeks of daily radiation, and five months of chemotherapy. I recall my first visit to the surgeon who would determine the recommendation for treatment. I was frightened, of course, but steeled myself to a bravery I knew I couldn't do without. Hysteria, of the sort I was used to during my nightmare visions, seemed almost as dangerous as the cancer itself. I asked in a fairly controlled tone of voice, I think, what the long-term effect of surgery on my breast would be. How deep would the cut be? Would it look like half a breast, or just a breast with a hole in it? The young woman surgeon, who was immensely capable and immensely busy, felt around for a few minutes, trying to distinguish the original lump from all the surrounding swellings that were the result of the various biopsies, then stepping away from me she said: "The breast [the medical people always said "the breast" and "your cancer," a choice of vocabulary that tended to reinforce a sense of guilt for having cancer in the first place] will look somewhat though not dramatically different. But you," and she pointed at me somewhere between my face and my heart, "will probably never be the same again."

And she was completely right about that. The immediate result was that I was no longer depressed, absolutely certain that I wanted to live as long as possible. The fears not only remained but became even more intense and with their increasing intensity, my increasing desire to escape them by facing them once and for all. Having a life-threatening illness not only changes perspective, as everyone says, but pattern. The relations between things seem to shift. Previously veiled or disguised connections are suddenly exposed, and as in fiction, it is the connection between seemingly disparate experiences that penetrates defenses and promises lucidity. Perhaps, that is why so many writers who undergo such an experience must write about it before they can resume writing anything else. Just as, despite great inner resistance, I do now. It seems absolutely necessary to name the change, and to do so, one has to become clear as to what led up to it, what came before.

Perhaps I had feared breast cancer even more than most women because my mother died of metastasized breast cancer when she was thirty-eight and I seven, and this experience, of witnessing her illness, decline, and death over some years, as well as the particular aftermath of the death constructed by a fairly insane family, had literally determined the structure of much of my life. Although I often felt embarrassed by the recognition that this period of childhood still influenced me forty-five years later, I know for certain now that every important experience I have ever had, everyone I've loved or hated, every central choice I've made — my marriage, my mothering, my friendships, my worst faults, my steadiest virtues, and certainly my writing — has been affected by this incident at the heart of the narrative of my life.

Years ago, I came to believe I had resolved old feelings about my mother through a combination of psychotherapy and writing, that I had transcended the legacy of loss, grief, and the threat of madness I knew as a child. I had written books about mothers, including myself, and books about daughters, all of them, according to Gloria, a therapist I worked with for about twelve years, written in part to bring my mother back to life. All of them, in that sense, were failures to me; yet all of them also were stepping stones away from her influence, each book like a stone across a rushing stream that periodically rises to overflow the banks, but each stone solid in its hard, flat existence.

After about six years of therapy and two more books, Gloria told me she thought I had finally buried my mother, and she had reason to think so. Strengthened by Gloria's kindness, frankness, and the carefully honed intuition of one who has made listening into an art, I had come to understand that I suffered from a sense of guilt for my mother's death, a guilt constructed of false but apparently typical childish beliefs about the omnipotence of wishes and the dark attraction of desolation and longing, if those emotions are all that continues to connect one to what has been lost. Death was a place, I had decided as a child, where my mother still lived, and I had grown into my forties when I understood that my love/hate relation to death, and the need to relive and relive my early powerful emotional ambivalence toward my mother's memory as well as her absence, had influenced my entire life story, rubbing it, slowly scraping away at it, polishing it at times to a magnetic and scintillating shine — just like the rushing stream upon those flat, safe stones. Achieving this understanding, I lived through periods of exhilarating well-being, the strongest sense of confidence and ordinary happiness I have ever known. I *had* finally buried my mother, in a way. What I did not fully appreciate then, but know for certain now, is the inevitability, with certain bedrock mythologies in a life, of periodic resurrection, or, to sustain the previous metaphor, of storm and flood.

Stories of our lives often happen by accident, and these stories provide the conditions, if one so chooses, to re-examine the past in a new and deeper way. Having breast cancer was such an experience for me. It followed a period during which all my central stories seemed to be about loss. The stories of loss began when Gloria herself died from metastasized breast cancer; continued with the slow dying and eventual death of Douglas's brother Simeon from A I D S; with immense work disappointments for both Douglas and me; and with an experience of prolonged anxiety during a trip Khary took to Jamaica that included a short but complete breakdown in myself.

I am sitting in Gloria's office, in my old chair, only this time I am the only one in the room as Gloria has been dead for some weeks. I have been here for over an hour, thinking and writing, and finally I close my notebook, get up, and for the last time walk out the double doors into the tiny garden that leads up the stairs to the street. I feel no sense of closure or resolution. Quite the opposite. I realize it will be some time before I comprehend what I have lost or even clarify what I may be able to preserve.

After the funeral, I had called her husband, also a therapist whose office was at the other end of the basement level of the brownstone they shared, and made an appointment to see him to talk about our mutual loss and get his advice about seeing another therapist, possibly someone Gloria herself might have recommended if she'd had the time. He and I decided I would put off the decision about entering therapy with someone else until I had thought about — in his words — what I had accomplished with Gloria. After all, I had "terminated" the first, long cycle of treatment some time ago, and now came back only for periodic epilogues, lasting months or weeks, motivated either by crises I needed help with, or simply by the desire to see her and engage in that special sort of conversation about the self that is possible with a long-known and beloved therapist. Her husband, who was obviously deeply bereaved, made a generous and surprising offer that day. I could, he said, come to sit in her room whenever I wished over the next few weeks. I could just call ahead and let him know I was coming, and no one would disturb me.

I went twice. The first time I sat in her chair, hoping to experience in some immutable material form the idea, which she had voiced on the occasion of various separations, that she would always be with me. I found her glasses on the windowsill near her chair where she always kept them, half-glasses to put on so she could read, and for a few moments, I put them on my own face. Then, her presence became very strong, as if she still inhabited the room — with her wide skirts, paisley button-up blouses, her flat shoes — as if even now she was shifting heavily in that chair, beneath me. She would look off into the distance, trying to find words that did not always seem to come easily to her, although insight did, as if she were able, like a painter or a dancer, to know things without language. The first time I began by just looking around the familiar place where I had undergone a transformation in my character, a sea change, Gloria called it, that began with a breakdown in my thirties when I reached my mother's death age. Twelve years later, sitting in Gloria's chair trying to comprehend the loss of her, a strange feeling overtook me. First I felt a heavy warmth, a heaviness that suggested an anchoring, or a sucking down, a hypnotic and familiar fatigue that threatens both consciousness and capacity, making me want to stop, give up, relinquish, retreat, a feeling I had described many times to Gloria of wanting to die. Then, as often happened, anxiety replaced fatigue, and I thought she was in the room and wanted me to get out of her chair. Bereavement. The wish to die to be reunited with the one who has been lost. The dangerous and compelling retreat from energy. And then the fear that such a wish might be granted. "She," or what I kept of her, protected me. I got up and resumed my old seat, opening a small black notebook in which I began to record all the feelings I'd had up to that moment. A feeling of calm returned, a sense of belonging.

The second time I visited her room, I decided to write a careful description of all its details so that in years to come they would not be lost to me. I sat down immediately in "my" chair, in reality the one I shared with many others, and as I had done hundreds of times before, I looked around at the peaceful yet provocative space she had created.

Each week there would be fresh flowers in a vase on her desk. Now there were dried flowers in the vase, purple roses. Perhaps she had put them there before she left this room for good, and here they remained, drying into another sort of beauty.

On the polished floor are two warm rugs, one brown tweed, the other green, brown, and yellow patterns of branches and flowers, a pattern I studied for many hours over the years when I regularly visited this room. The yellow couch I never lay down on because I always wanted to face her was behind me as usual, and I got up and lay down on it then, just to feel what might have been. Rising, I felt, like a blow to the chest, the emptiness of her black leather chair, the chair now filled with her absence. I recall the same odd, powerful tangibility of absence in my father's chair after his death. For months it did not seem ordinary, but always empty, as if emptiness and absence were things you could touch, be touched by, embrace, and, if you had nothing else, preserve.

On her chairside table are her old, scratchy notes in two spiral notebooks. I remember her picking them up and beginning to write only when I was reporting dreams, as if she could recall everything else adequately but needed notes to remember the intricate images of the unconscious. If my dream was short and clear, as some dreams are a perfect distillation of a broad pattern of feeling, she would write only the beginning, then take her glasses off her nose and look at me. This would happen each time I had the recurring dream about the heart in the cave. I was walking down a windswept, desolate but peaceful ocean beach and I would come to a large cave. Inside, I was burying something, packing it down with sand. When I was done I said aloud, I have buried my heart and I will never take it out again. So, what exactly have you buried there? she would ask each time, making a note on her page, then staring into my eyes.

On the table on the other side of her chair are the objects I have studied so often, whenever I needed to look away from her. A small sculpture I believe I have seen somewhere else, known in some other place, of a woman's face with a beaded headdress in bronze. A tiny man in coat and hat, head down, running, escaping from something. An ancient Hindu goddess raising her many hands. Over the fireplace, with its magnificent Mexican tiles, an old rabbi with a long white beard and a cap painted black looks eternally into his open book. On the wall, a woman made of white stone swings freely in a hammock — or she is the hammock — her arms raised behind her, her body a V shape as she swings. And framed in gold, there is a detail of a Reubens, the very same portrait I had on my wall as a child, which still hangs in my study today, reminding me of the inexplicable connection I felt to this woman whose heart was remarkably open to the stories of mine. Occasionally, we meet people who seem like lost kin or spiritual siblings. Some might say we'd known each other in a past life and were destined to know each other in successive lives as well. A very comforting story that both recognizes the mysteriousness at the heart of certain unlikely loves and suggests that terrible loss is not irretrievable, that there are future meetings with lost beloveds the nature of which we cannot imagine. "What is death like?" I asked another close friend who had recently died and then came to me in a dream. She responded, "near, very near."

Gloria's books and papers are still in place, and remembering the pain of dismantling my father's apartment, my old home, after his death when I was twenty-eight years old, I wonder when her husband and children will take this room apart, with its crowds of shadow selves in pain, in moments of reparation and hours of healing under Gloria's careful, respectful, and pragmatic eye.

She lied to me twice, but her trustworthiness had taken firm root by the time I knew of the lies, and so I am left with regret and dismay rather than anger. The first was about her illness. I had asked her if she were ill several weeks before she died. She looked weak and gray and something clearly was wrong. She said she was fine, was having some minor blood problem but would be okay. The second lie was about the illness of her child. After she died, I found out from her husband that one of their children had diabetes, as does my older son, and moreover, they had contracted the disease about the same time. I suppose in both instances she felt too vulnerable herself to risk my reactions threatening what must have been a precarious balance at the time. If she were here I would say, You should have told me. As she is not, my criticisms are greatly outweighed by my love.

At her funeral it was said that she loved Bach, a serene and orderly music. We had talked a great deal of our mutual need for order, and although I do not know her history in relation to this appreciation, I know that mine came into existence in her room because of what she taught me. When I met her, I was besieged by passions I did not understand and by a belief held in place since childhood that only passion could rule my life authentically. Over the course of a decade, she helped me to understand that I could control my life, my surroundings, and my emotions. I came to see that I did not have to be a slave to impulse, immersed in chaos in order to distinguish myself from the myth of an orderly, disciplined mother, with her carefully created, elegant outfits and her formal dining room, which I was allowed to enter only when she and the other grown-ups were ready for dessert. It took many years to accomplish it, but under Gloria's guidance I became not only capable of but fascinated with order, structure, and design in seemingly every aspect of my life. I was reading many biographies of women writers during that period, and in one on the life of George Eliot I found the phrase, used by Eliot in a letter about her own search for control, "the self that self restrains."* This idea became ideal for me, an aspect of character I was determined either to recover or to create. Compared to my passion in this search, naming the old heart lying buried in that cave seemed an uninteresting task, or at least one that could be put off for an indefinite time. After I had breast cancer, I would be forced to return to the cold, gray beach where I would have to uncover that beating thing, whatever it was, from its place under the damp ground. But Gloria had returned or given to me the equally important possession of discipline, and this treasure was rich enough to sustain me with emotional and intellectual work for many years.

The last time I saw her she was lying in a hospital bed

* Ruby Virginia Redinger, *George Eliot: The Emergent Self* (New York: Knopf, 1975).

in her living room, preparing for death. I lay down next to her and we embraced. I said I loved her and she said, this time directly, with no analytic questions about my need to know her feelings, that she loved me too. She said she was worried about me, losing another "mother" to breast cancer, and I promised her I would be all right. I meant that I would not become a slave to grief, as I had as a child. Yet, because of the multiple losses I was to experience in the next few years, I would break my promise, and when I had breast cancer myself, I would long for her voice, her wise face smiling ruefully at the accidents of life. I would miss her with the physical immediacy one feels in the early months following a death. I would see her walking down 94th Street.

She said she did not want to die, but was not afraid to die. I try to imagine myself so centered, focused, and brave and find it impossible. I always fear the end of things. Leaving anything behind, even painful experience, is difficult. Several friends have told me I should write something else now, not immerse myself in these griefs again. But this is the only way I know to find the next flat stone that might be wide enough to hold me for awhile.

Gloria believed without question, as so many do, as I once confidently did, in the importance of personal stories. "Your way of writing," she used to call my work. When we talked of writing, my resistance and loss of desire to write, the seeming futility of trying to affect an oblivious world, she seemed more than at any other time, confused. And we would go back to our digging — to the older sorrows, my father's judgments, my mother's leavings. I would see my writing as a way to gain their attention, to do magic and negate even death. I would swing between grief and hope, like the white stone woman end-lessly swinging on Gloria's wall. First, I would dream of bearing shabby gifts no one wanted, of dinners poorly prepared, raw chicken, insufficient amounts. Then I'd write something that expressed what I felt or understood about experience, and I would feel worthy again, a giver to the world.

When I walked into her room that last time, having been met by a nurse in the waiting room who solemnly ushered me upstairs to the part of the house where the family lived, where of course I had never been, I resisted clarity with a terrified vengeance. "Oh, how beautiful," I virtually sung as I sat down on a chair looking around the spacious room, as if she were not lying in a hospital bed, drawn and pale, obviously nearly unable to move. "I am dying, Jane," she said to me, and that was when I began to cry, rose from my seat across from her, and lay down next to her on her bed. When I left she told me we would see each other again, have time to say good-bye. But when I reached the stairs and looked back at her, a familiar and awful light filled the room, a light I have seen at other deathbeds and dreamed of many times. It is not a light that clarifies in the ordinary sense. Rather, it illuminates, it glows with a kind of shimmering fog.

Several days later, her husband called to say she had died. "I felt I would never see her again," I said. "And now that has come to pass," he responded.

I did see her once more, in her coffin, but that is when a face seems closed, a mask, the spirit gone.

What did you accomplish with Gloria in your work over all those years? I have heard her husband's question again and again in the past six months since I have begun writing this story as part of an effort to recover more fully from a disease that kills by overflowing boundaries and devouring once delineated body parts into itself.

She taught me I could trust that I knew what was happening to me and around me, that I too had what I so loved in her, the gift of clarity. She taught me that confusion and chaos themselves could be a defense against clarity because of fear of pain or rage.

Gloria and I were aligned in our efforts to save, love, but also control, a desperate and hungry part of myself. We cradled her, but we took her in hand. Twelve years later the part of me that gained strength and reality in her office feels like myself, not merely some theatrical mask or plastic prosthesis intended to support and protect the damaged stump, scarred and ugly, beneath. Yet I see that in a way I have been talking of masks all along, of familiar, trusted but still constructed limbs. Burials are never endings. I should have learned that from the many deaths I have known. I have become a woman whose world is not always beyond her control. But now I must retrieve — as Gloria knew but died before she could help me with the hauling — some of what I buried during those years.

There is a painting on the wall of my new therapist's office. A sequence of arches seems to lead to various tunnels that become darker and darker as they move back from the surface. Those are the corridors I have become afraid of, the places of extremity I so wanted to leave behind. For months the sounds were loud but indecipherable, the darkness not opaque enough to block out threatening shadows. They moved across my vision all day as I rearranged my eating habits toward a diet of fruits and vegetables, rearranged my days to include walking several miles at a brisk pace. And all the while, like some dedicated farmer gathering crops before the rains, I garnered my strength for the next treatment.

Now, the treatments over, I am still in those corridors. The darkness is lifting and it is not so scary all the time. I picture myself walking slowly down the shaded, cool cloisters until I am in a kind of courtyard. The ground is windswept and dusty. The trees are bare, and I am alone. The emotions are so extreme they might engulf me and everyone I know. And so I must sit and stare for some time, allowing the waves of feeling to pass through me. But there is no going back, nor would I want to. Here is the place I have been trying to find since the long depression began.

There is a passage in the novel by Jane Hamilton, *A Map of the World*, which I transcribed into my journal:

I used to think that bravery involved action. It took courage, I figured, to move forward, to pursue a dream, to get ahead in the world. Just to get where you were supposed to. I thought having desire took courage. Now I realize that none of that requires bravery. The only thing you really need bravery for is standing still. For standing by.

And this one, from "Telling Stories under Siege," by Amos Oz:

His stories might have been every bit as terrifying as the besieging reality out there. In fact, his stories might even have had more terror in them than the wood or the bush in the dark, his monsters more monstrous, his spirits more evil, his ices more frozen, his fires more blazing. Yet in the stories, the horror was caught in words and the demons were contained by form.

If my fear is that feelings can grow like cancer—chaotic, devouring, and deadly—and the safety of boundary is all that can keep me alive, then it must be a good thing that I have begun this narrative: a search in language for some intuited subtext beneath the ordinary disorder of a life. There is a definite chaos in my journals as the pages mount up.

In my sessions with Aaron, my new therapist, I try to see patterns by listening for the crucial interruptions that may suggest a meaning to experience beyond the partial vision of my consciousness. I am brave enough to walk the corridors because of the rules of the trade. I am protected by the walls beyond which secrets must not be spoken, and by a relationship whose formal definition is as strict as its capacity to permit intimate revelation hopes to be limitless. More than these, I am brave in reaction to his kindness, capacity for attention, and respect. In this combination lies the humility I believe to be essential upon entering the terrain of another person's interior life, however confident the theory that describes and interprets in a general way.

And here, in these pages, I shape and reshape the structure, the language. On the printed draft I design new connections and more precise descriptions with a dark black pen. Frequently, my newest, best insights are made in the margins, between the lines, continuing onto the back of the page. Then, on this computer, I work them into the text as if they had always been there. Something shifts inside me. I am saved by form.

A Sense of Threat

I am trying to understand one experience by what it shares with another. Patterns come to me, clusters of memories that seem to belong together, and I cannot, simply for the sake of ease or sequence, keep them apart. Old memories of the months preceding and the early years after my mother's death when I was seven years old. A panic attack I experienced when Khary was attending a semester abroad, months before the cancer cells won their battle with my immune system and hardened into a tumor. And chemotherapy, which so frightened me I could write neither the word nor the name of the doctor in my journal but had to resort to initials, or watch my barely manageable fears escalate out of control.

I will not perceive the connections among these memories until all the cancer treatments are done. But I am dreaming with vague knowledge of being ashamed, and the shame is always for needing something I cannot have, or something that is not what I thought it to be. Somehow, I am humiliated, not merely disappointed; exposed, not merely wrong. A little beggar girl I saw long ago in a poverty-stricken street in Naples is in my kitchen. She looks at me with the pathetic eyes of a hungry cat and scratches on my refrigerator door with dirty, bitten nails. A river fills with blood, and long-missing bodies float to the surface while I sit in a boat aloof, even dissociated, wondering at the strangeness of what is happening right before my eyes. A distanced critic, I watch the dramas and keep track of all of the themes.

Now, I turn back the pages of my journal to the day I found the lump, a surprisingly undifferentiated hardness I wasn't even sure was a lump at first. I read my brief entry the day I went for a needle biopsy and received the diagnosis. "You are the fifth person I have diagnosed with breast cancer this morning," the radiologist said to me, and it was only noon. "It's an epidemic."

But eight months before that, when I was experiencing increasingly intense panic attacks, I had written: I feel as if an actual illness inhabits me. Something at once foreign and part of me devouring myself.

I appreciate the danger of ascribing facile metaphor to illness, especially to cancer. I can become angry at the many books and acquaintances who advise one to move to northern Maine, where a hypnotic serenity presumably neutralizes the effect of sorrow and loss, to subsist on brown rice and seaweed, or "eliminate stress" from one's life (an injunction that only increases stress in me, as I become stressed by the thought of how much stress there is in my life). I am suspicious of alternative healing methods that overemphasize the "spiritual" core of physical illness and even counsel an avoidance of Western medical knowledge. My life has been saved by Western medicine, an early, relatively small cancerous tumor removed from my breast, followed by harsh chemical treatments that have hopefully destroyed any cancer cells that might have been left behind.

But there is a sense one gains irrevocably after a life-threatening illness, that the mind, or spirit, and body are indeed one, or at least in intimate communion. I believe in the reality of the spirit and that it can be hurt as well as healed. For me, that healing always involves various forms of storytelling—the kind you recount to a therapist in that space out of ordinary space and time out of ordinary time called a "session"; the kind you write and rewrite in various formulations, experimenting with various designs; the kind you dream. It is in the percep-

tion of design that I experience healing, and if that word
has been rolled around too often by shallow minds seeking instant and painless transformation so that it has lost
its original power to suggest the relief of remedy, the
joy of cure, I find that I still remain attached to its old-
fashioned, simple promise that what is broken can, at
least sometimes, be repaired.

Between chemotherapy treatments are three weeks during which I try to make myself as strong as possible in
body and mind, not only to prepare myself for what is
a terrifying encounter each time but to build up my immune system in the face of attack. Close friends offer
love and gifts, and one of the most treasured is the gift of
several weeks' stay in Bellport, Long Island, at the home
of my friends, Sally and Bill, who are traveling in China.
Reading or sleeping in these large, quiet rooms where
all day and into twilight the sun alters the pale off-white
colors of the walls, reflecting rosy pink, pale green, a
slightly bluish lavender; swimming in the backyard pool,
which is surrounded by hedges, maple, pine, and at one
end, an old grape arbor; walking the hilly roads to the
bay, or biking to the tiny, quiet town, I am at the same
time veiled and wide opened, thinking I am perfectly
composed, like an elegantly constructed story, then suddenly overwrought, bursting into unfocused tears. I am
extremely frightened of cars that, in New York City and
here in these quiet streets, seem always about to crash
into me, and I leap out of their way as they pass, causing
drivers to look at me as if I am slightly mad. My need for
love and reassurance is gigantic. I try to keep it on a short
leash, afraid I will lose any hope of forbearance. Fear of
death races through me like a brush fire, indistinguish-
able from the hot flashes that have greatly intensified

since I stopped taking estrogen the day of the diagnosis, so that one sets off the other by association and it all comes back, weeks of being trapped in my body, its pain, its disease, the certainty of its inevitable disintegration. The only escape is into the details of management.

Chemotherapy changes the body in many small and obvious, as well as large and mysterious, ways, and for the first time in my life I have a skin rash due to the chemicals in sunscreen lotion or to the sun itself. I use #15 to protect myself but spend large amounts of time wondering if I should escalate to #45 or return to #8. I plan my meals of spinach, broccoli, brown rice, count off a small pile of vitamins each morning. Despite my undiminished craving for hamburgers, vodka on ice, cigarettes, bread and cheese, I research and create a dozen vegetable dishes and I eat them. I eat them every day and I follow them with glasses of clear, purified water. Despite my desire to sit and stare, read or think or write, I walk, and I walk fast. And despite a lifelong ambivalent love affair with death, I have never been so certain that I want to live as long as I possibly can. During the months of treatment, the clearest reason for living is to see Adam and Khary develop their lives, their children born, their ambitions fulfilled, not to have to leave them. Only much later will the desire to live include the wish to see my own life develop. Now, hope is only sought after, not yet reclaimed.

I buy new sneakers for my daily walks, thick-soled, high-tops. I list the treatment dates, crossing off numbers 1 and 2, beginning the process I will continue for the next four months and beyond, of writing everything down to keep myself from succumbing to panic. But I am frequently in a state of fear. If Douglas is more than fifteen minutes late, I begin to cry with the grief of a child abandoned, incapacitated and alone, and when he returns from a run, a trip to the store, a little late from work, I sometimes have to turn my back on him, close a door behind me, hide my shame.

I try to love my body, take care of it, look at it in the mirror despite its ordinary signs of aging and the not so ordinary long indentation on the side of my right breast. But often, it doesn't feel like mine. It has been cut into, entered, poisoned by strangers. These assaults, I am warned in printed releases I have to sign, may have unpredictable consequences to my heart, my liver, although I am assured that "probably" everything will be fine. But I am suddenly aware of my body parts as if they are delicate infants needing my protection, part of myself and apart from myself at the same time: my liver, my heart.

One night Douglas and I make love, the first time since the surgery, and just as I knew would happen the moment he is inside me I begin to cry. Not so much cry as keen. I sound like a woman in mourning, a low wail to the heavens as she watches a coffin descend. I hear my own voice as if from far away, as I did when I was in the hardest part of labor, giving birth to my sons. In the past months of this lonely journey, I have seen how I cherish beyond measure the old love between Douglas and me. But ordinary vocabulary does not suffice. Old implies worn, or even worn out, but I mean it in the sense of an heirloom, precious, reliable, rich with history. People say I am strong, but he has seen the fear, knows how many nights we have slept with the light on, held me when my sobs seemed bottomless, listened quietly, at times holding his head in his hands while he looks at me sadly, to my shouts of rage at the American medical system, at rude nurses and doctors who are afraid of pain and suffering, at tumors that are over one centimeter and so require chemotherapy as a treatment that perhaps, but not definitely, might stop the spread of what, I am informed repeatedly, is a systemic disease. Otherwise, I would have told them to cut the breast off, take it, I would have said, and leave me be. When he gently lays his fingers against my wounded breast or touches the still partly numb right arm, I think of blood, of vomit, of the terror of losing my hair, which I've been assured will not happen with the particular combination of chemicals being injected into me. When he moves inside me I lay my hand on my own hair as if by pressing down I might keep it rooted there, and I am lost somewhere inside my body which is vast, foreign, yet some poor fragile thing. Then in the next moment I fill it again and know the difference between his touching and entering me and all of them touching me, entering me, actually entering the flesh of my breast and cutting away tissue for testing, for saving my life, yes, but cutting parts away, parts I have never seen myself but picture as throbbing, raw, and I am unable to say how hard it has been and how dearly I love him because my need is bottomless, it will swallow us both. And so I surround myself with layers of his silence until I am inside it and can feel the words he might have been able to say at some other time, in some other life. Nor does he cry with me, but tonight I am reconciled to this habitual absence of words and in the darkness of the room, against the comforting, damp sheets, after awhile I am able to say it, it has been so hard, and to repeat it and repeat it as if this simple phrase is a baptism, or a burial song.

The next morning, Ruthie, oldest intimate of my soul, arrives with her dog, Puto. We walk the narrow streets leading toward and away from the bay, talking of our lives, pressing constantly for some deeper knowledge framed in words that will enable us to escape the demons of depression and fear we have so often faced and fled together. I consider her very brave, and often dream of her exploring remote islands I am frightened to visit because of dangers lurking in ocean storms, or in the broad deserts she and her daughter are willing to cross in order to swim in some perfect lagoon. She dreams of me and the places I have lived as havens she comes upon when she is lost. Accompanied by her dog, an exceptionally intelligent animal whose only fault is that he barks incessantly when he's excited, which he always is on long walks, we wander around roads leading to mansions surrounded by gardens, expansive lawns and high hedges that make Sally's spacious and comfortable home seem like a functional cottage. As we walk we talk of love and need, and then she says, after a characteristic silence in which I know she is pondering some thought until she finds the precise words, "You have a great need for love, to receive it and to give it," and the trapdoor snaps open. I have to stop and catch my breath. I am standing at the edge of the darkness. The way down is steep. I am flushed with hot shame. I am the beggar girl with catlike paws. "No I don't," I say to her, a child's voice, as if I've been insulted and have no sensible response. "What's wrong with it?" she says. We are stopped on the road. Puto is barking at us as if he is a sheepdog and we are his wandering sheep. "What's wrong with it?" she repeats. But all I am able to say is, "I don't know. Something is wrong with it. I know that much." I am filled with images shooting through my brain like some video rewinding, spinning its pictures backward in time.

It is eight months earlier, the previous fall, shortly after Khary had gone to live and study in Jamaica for a semester abroad. I begin to experience panic attacks when I don't hear from him every few days. (He cannot get a phone installed for several months, and so I have to wait for him to communicate with us from pay phones, which are not very numerous in Kingston.) He is reliable and generous about calling me far more frequently than most grown children will call their mothers. Nevertheless, about a day before he is due to call I become obsessed with disaster fantasies so vivid I sometimes have to ward them off verbally, talking back to old demons, often out loud while walking down the street.

After several weeks of this, I consult a famous therapist on the recommendation of a friend who is a therapist herself. Over the course of about four weeks, for reasons I will never fully know, this woman frightens me, hurts me, and weakens me even more than I already am. She interprets my relationships with my sons critically, casting me as an overbearing, intrusive, and deeply hostile mother, a very bad mother indeed. Being fairly sophisticated about psychotherapy, its theory and practice, I twice try to defend myself, questioning her interpretations, and twice she acknowledges that she has been too harsh, apologizes, and even wonders out loud if she, a woman who does not have biological children, is too "child-identified" herself. Then she does it again. What is astonishing to me is that I do not leave immediately but remain for a month. I will never again underestimate the power of therapists, the vulnerability of patients, even the least naive. It's a dangerous business — this putting your life in the hands of a stranger — an action not to be done carelessly, or without restraint. There are ways in which I like her, of course, and keep hoping that with Gloria gone I have found someone new to help me through recurring bouts of depression and anxiety, of which these panic attacks are the worst symptoms I've experienced in years.

After some weeks, I describe her and the things she is

saying to me to Leona, who is very knowledgeable about therapy herself and who becomes furious in my behalf. As soon as she begins raging at the therapist's stupidity, callousness, and downright wrongness, insisting that my sons are not only strong but devoted to me, not only "separate" in their own lives (that most overriding proof of "good mothering") but also profoundly connected to Douglas and to me (which few seem to value much at all), I understand that she is right, that I am being broken down by this strange and in some ways likable woman who for some reason dislikes me or is unbalanced by me, and that I can never return to her. I call her and tell her just this, and when she does not bill me for the sessions, I take it as an acknowledgment that she has been wrong.

Nevertheless, her accusations take root. My capacity for belief in disaster regarding my children is thoroughly tied to my fear that I have been a "bad mother," just as my surely once more malleable and ordinary belief in my badness as a child had been hardened, as if with gravel mixed into clay, by my mother's death and the circumstances surrounding it.

One day when I was seven years old and my sister four, we were sent away to an aunt's home, and when we returned two or three days later, our mother was gone. Gone for good. Her clothing had been cleaned out of the closets and distributed to Goodwill, or to relatives and friends. The suede and leather purses I played with, changing black for blue as she changed her elegant outfits for each day's work; the collection of artificial roses, violets, and lilies she wore in her lapels; and the stack of flowered embroidered handkerchiefs — all were gone. My father must have snatched one from the clutches of whoever was dispensing with her physical presence with such efficient dispatch, because I found one among his things when he died, and I still have it, a pattern of pink roses on a background of white, folded among the few mementos I have of her. No doubt they believed her children would be better off not witnessing the awesome dismantling that occurs after a death, as they believed, with such mistaken certainty, that we would be better off not attending the funeral. We returned to a house empty of our mother and much of what she had personally possessed.

The household she had created around her remained, however: the expensive furniture, the pale green china, the cut-crystal inkstand that sat on a graceful silver tray. She was a successful businesswoman, my father a barely paid radical activist, and over the years, with my father in charge of housekeeping and money scarce, possessions grew shabbier. A green velvet armchair that had been her favorite place to sit fell apart and disappeared. We began to use yellow plates bought in the corner hardware store for dinners that now were informal family affairs more suited to my father's working-class background and tastes than the carefully served meals of several courses, restricted to the two of them, my mother had preferred. The crystal inkstand looked more and more anachronistic on its bookshelf, surrounded by my father's dusty half-torn books on Marx, Lenin, and Soviet fiction. When my father died, and we were grown, we pulled it out from the back of the grimy shelf and gave it to my cousin, whose house and housekeeping standards would properly show it off.

But through all those years, I remained haunted by the question—where did she go? I could not comprehend the finality of her absence, and since ours was not a religious family, there was no shared mythology to attempt an explanation. I developed the idea that if I kept a close enough vigil, thinking of her every minute, I could bring her back.

At times, it seemed I was successful. A few years later, when I was in the fifth grade and a school monitor, I watched a thin, dark-haired, elegantly dressed woman kiss her child good-bye near my post at an outside door. But then, probably made uncomfortable by my relentless staring and conspiratorial smiles, she began taking leave of her son farther down the block where I could only glimpse her outline in the sun. And so I realized it hadn't been my mother after all, come back to watch over me, although, for mysterious reasons, having to pretend she was the mother of somebody else. I returned to my more controllable fantasies of her ghostly presence in my room, behind her photograph on my wall, or within my own skin.

When my vigil failed, if I thought of other things or other loves too long, I was responsible for her remaining dead, I believed, just as my desperate need of relief from her dying by hoping for her death had hastened her end. I had killed her. I was guilty of this terrible thing. Throughout my life this belief will surface, then descend into a distant shadow again. But the distancing is never remote enough to destroy my sense of culpability, the threat of punishment lurking close behind.

There were lies that reinforced both guilt and connection, the most dangerous being the idea that I looked exactly like her, was exactly like her. For a child it was an easy piece of syntactical magic to edit out the like. I was her, except that, like many mythical heroines, I had to pay a steep price for my power. She was so beautiful that people stared when she walked into a room, so brilliant she could manage a career as a successful businesswoman while still doing courageous, clandestine political work, and she possessed an indefinable and awe-inspiring quality called *dignity* I could never fully comprehend, although it seemed to have something to do with keeping your feelings under control (mine were notoriously intense, a characterization I responded to with both pride and shame), and not becoming overpowered by your sexual desires. I developed a life-shaping ambivalence to this identification, wanting to be her and thus somehow with her again, but also wanting to be different from her in order not to be dead. It was a false mythology. I recently saw an old film of her, made only one or two years before she died, and I was reminded that I didn't resemble her any more than the average child. If my interests and talents are any sign, I am not like her in temperament or character either. She was an elegant woman, deeply concerned with appearances, whose need for personal success was evidently as great as her need for love. It was my father whose passions were tropical, humid. He sweated when he was thrilled with some piece of music, actually salivated visibly when he was reunited with an old, beloved friend. He longed for my sister and me with unashamed grief when we were growing up and trying to get away from him. He gave us, whenever we asked, and when we did not, anything and everything he had.

Another sort of lie—more specific, concrete, but equally effective for my self-blaming purposes: she died not of cancer but of a "slipped disc." This distortion was perpetrated by my father while she was still alive so that I wouldn't speak the terrible word, cancer, in her presence. But several weeks before her last hospitalization, I had called to her in the night after waking from a nightmare. I heard her call back to me, shouting my name, not a comforting, maternal response but a cry of pain of her own and then I heard a crash. She had tried to get out of bed and come to me, it turned out, but her bones were already weakened by disease and when her legs could not hold her, she had fallen onto the floor. For the next ten years I remained convinced that her fall, in response to my need, was the cause of the slipped disc that killed her. This narrative itself was a distillation, of course, a representation of deeper, more complex stories, classic tales of childish rage at the withdrawal, even into illness, of a parent, especially a mother; of the influence of gender and emerging sexuality on such a wish when the father is beloved too, magnetic and powerful; of the wicked wish that the abandoning mother who is too weakened and frail to pay attention to children and their needs would be punished and die. And then there are the particularities of history, less generic, harder to unravel when the time comes. For this was a mother whose leavings began long before the final leaving, so the daughter's longing was covered over by resentment and anger long before the final anger would become entrenched, veiling the longing that seemed to form the center, which felt at times like an absence, of her life.

Easily, comfortably, I slip into the third person. Even old passions fill me with mysterious shame. Yet I believe that I must find the courage to write the story of that short, threatening breakdown as a chapter in this grief narrative, this cancer journal, must say in words again this piece of self-knowledge I learned almost talmudically with Gloria, going over it and over it, layering it with interpretations and associations, yet forgot and forget, again and again. I believe that what I love will be destroyed. I was a bad girl and my mother died. If I am a bad mother (and what mother is not a bad mother in additioɪi to whatever and whomever else she is; the evidence can always be found) disaster will take my children.

On a Wednesday afternoon, there is a call on my telephone machine from the long-distance operator in Kingston, Jamaica, but no one is home and as the call is collect, Khary is not permitted to leave a message: an ordinary event that takes on extraordinary ramifications for me as soon as it happens. He was trying to call because of some emergency but couldn't get through, I decide. It is that simple, the moment that swift. A call that, at another time, might have had no effect. A moment that, in ordinary time, would have moved into the past like other moments, instead of exploding into dark smoke that remains in the air, stuck to the walls, permeating my lungs, literally shortening my breath for days. Ordinary time fractures for me, and I become an inadequate vessel for past and present, dangerously enmeshed. The idea that something is wrong takes hold and I cannot loosen it for the next four days. The only defense I have, besides talking for hours to Leona on the phone, is writing. I write a part of a chapter for the book I am working on—an orderly, interpretive piece of nonfiction—and I still don't know how I managed to accomplish this task except that it suggests the genuine change that has taken place in my years of work with Gloria. The self that self restrains might be fragile at times, but at least she is not entirely illusory. And I write in my journal, where no restraint is required, every hour of every day.

While I am writing, I begin to feel a slight faith that he is really okay, but the faith is as ungraspable as light. I cannot gather it, or move into it, but only glimpse it as a reality next to me, from which I am somehow excluded. I only know that if I stop writing, even for a moment, I will be swept away by terror. So over and over I write down reminders of ordinary reality, signposts of ordinary time, as, less than a year later, I will do to mark the passage of weeks through chemotherapy and radiation that feel, also, like a punishment, a permanent hell that, because it is deserved, or at least destined, will never cease. I list all the late nights waiting for my sons when they return, happy and well, all the planes I thought would crash that landed safely, all the viruses that did not become some dread disease.

By Saturday morning I have cried for so many hours, pacing from one corner of our apartment to the other and back again, that Douglas has run out of sympathy and is becoming desperate and angry. I understand that I am making him feel utterly helpless, and that he is convinced I have the ability to control this madness and am refusing to do so out of some terrible self-indulgent need to over-dramatize my life. I try to come out of the terror, and I can't. Perhaps I am resisting my own best efforts in some banal need for punishment, but it feels like the opposite at the time: I am being punished for the extremity of my needs.

On Saturday night I call the Kingston, Jamaica, police station to find out if any Americans have been reported missing or murdered that week. The officer on duty is extremely pleasant, much more so than those at the 24th precinct in my neighborhood whom I have sometimes called with similar questions. No violence has been reported, the charming voice assures me. Nevertheless, I book flights to Jamaica for the coming Monday morning, just in case Khary hasn't called by Sunday night. In these mad actions and irrational plans I grope for and even find a bit of control. Finally, I call one of his professors, a number I have been given for emergencies, and although fearing Khary's anger if everything is indeed fine, I ask this man when he has last seen my son. He is as gracious as the cop, assuring me he is a parent too and understands my concerns. (But of course I am speaking to him in a normal voice, for the duration of the discussion suspending my wild tones.) He has seen him, alive and well, the previous Thursday, and although this fact undermines my theory that something disastrous happened Wednesday night when the phone message was left, it takes only a few minutes after hanging up for my panic to rise again.

I can hear my father's voice after my mother's death, pleading: Stop that crying, crying isn't going to bring her back, when my sobs and screams made him feel, no doubt, as helpless as Douglas does now. Behind my father's I hear my husband's sighs, even his breath, I imagine, furious and desperate. I listen to Leona's voice, reminding me that many losses are packed into this panic. I try to recall Gloria, literally call her up by reading old journal entries about her, and come across entry after entry describing her efforts to get me to look into the place where loss becomes abandonment and love turns murderous in its power to destroy. From that long-ago time, I try to reenter the present so I can achieve the "clarity of self-respect" she insists I deserve. But I have reached the point of no return. There is nothing between me and my savage terrors, my most vigilant obsessions, my weakest self.

When I am at the bottom, I realize that the panic itself has turned into grief, as if the worst has already happened. When I remind myself that I am frightened but really know nothing for sure, I am a little better for a few minutes, even an hour. But then the anxiety mounts back into terror and terror into grief. The future collapses with the past into the present moment where I sit alone in a room, conjuring up the image of a face until it is nearly solid flesh, keeping a ruthless vigil in my head.

Finally, late Sunday afternoon, Khary calls. He sounds normal, and why shouldn't he? He is normal. His life is normal. He said he would call by Sunday, and on Sunday he calls, so he figures his mother is normal too, and I certainly try to appear to be, instantly casting the tone of my voice into a false but familiar rhythm, as calm and low a cadence as I can manage.

We talk only a few minutes, and then I hand the phone to Douglas and leave the house to walk. I am exhausted and frightened. Anxiety remains at a low level for weeks, like muddy waters after a murderous flood. The self I re-encountered is ghostly, familiar, and powerful. I do not want to claim her, yet I am scared she is all I have ever really had. When I am diagnosed with breast cancer the following May, that ghostly other, that scratching cat-girl, is the self I fear most of all. During the week before surgery, and the harder weeks afterward, waiting through medical consultations and sleepless nights for a final diagnosis and treatment plan, I can become nearly paralyzed by the thought: What will I do if she gets out?

During the summer months I am not teaching, and between chemotherapy treatments I spend as much time as I can arrange near the water. Ruthie and I climb over huge white dunes striped with wide meadows of tall grass to reach a famously beautiful Wellfleet Bay. The tide is extremely low and large sandbars spotted with watery patches of seaweed and shell are visible. Walking over this damp, flat terrain, you can hardly tell where the land ends and water begins. Both appear to be brown, then blue, then brown again. The waves are tiny and gentle, a thin sheet of sparkling wetness over sand.

In the distance a couple emerges. They undress and walk for yards until the bay is deep enough to swim, and even out there it is so shallow that when they cease swimming and stand up, the water only reaches their thighs. I can see signs of age on their bodies, white hair, a slight roundness in their shoulders, a fleshiness in his chest, a boniness in hers. And then they embrace and kiss for some time—their aging bodies, the calm, shallow water—all of it comforts so deeply my legs feel weightless, my body fluid. I can walk for miles in my sturdy high-tops. I can fall into an easy sleep in the sand.

But at the ocean I am agitated, unsatisfied, afraid to risk the cold water even at low tide. I don't know how strict I must be about the sun, as the nurse was so casual and disinterested. "Oh well," she said over her shoulder while preparing vials and tubes, "best to avoid it altogether." But when I asked if I could sit in it for short periods, since I so love the beach, she said with equal casualness, "Oh sure, but best to wear a hat."

I am covered, forehead to ankle, with #15, a hat, an umbrella, and every tiny pain is a cause of anxiety as the days move inexorably toward Treatment Number 3. When I try to risk the water, the ocean I once adored, I am filled with fear of waves and tides. I cannot go in past my knees. Only months later, when all the treatments are finished and I reenter my ordinary life again, when my days are not marked by a number checked off on a page, will I dream that I am standing on a beautiful wooden dock, watching a brave young boy dive into dark, still water where the ocean meets the bay.

At times, as if with a poisonous fluid I cannot stop, I fill up with anger: at Ruthie for sudden small distances; at people on the beach for talking too loudly; at Douglas for remaining at the house and not loving the water as much as I do; at the ocean for being too cold, and the sun merciless. The only thing I don't feel angry at — but only theorize abstractly that surely there must be anger and it must be related to all these other angers — is the disease of cancer that has threatened my life. The week before, on television, I heard the famous breast surgeon, Susan Love, describe cancer treatments as "cut, poison, and burn." I have been cut, am in the midst of being poisoned, and have the burning yet to go, and when the cutting and poisoning and burning are done, I can be given no assurances that I shall not have to go through it all again. As long as I am "in treatment" I feel I "have" cancer, and cannot seem to fully grasp that the tumor has been cut out, the surrounding tissue and lymph nodes found to be free of disease, that the treatment, which I have seen nearly kill two close friends, is "merely preventative" and, compared to other harsher chemical combinations, "mild." Anger fills me and grows into rage all day and into the evening. I try to keep it at bay, but it gathers every small dark rivulet into itself. It swells. I should probably walk out into the hills where no one can hear me or be harmed by me and scream as loudly as I can. But I keep the screams within. I freeze, grow stiff. I snarl for breath.

At about midnight, in the back bedroom Douglas and I use, with its sheer white curtains, worn flowered wallpaper, old wooden chests painted dark maroon, my anger finally dissipates and now here at last is my fear, my plain terror of the real thing. And once again, although I have been sniping at him all day, Douglas takes pity on me and holds me until my shoulders descend, my spine curves out of its tight rigidity, my muscles loosen their grip on my neck, my fingers, my arches, the cat-girl slinks away, and I begin to fall asleep.

A heat wave covers the East Coast as it does almost every summer for several weeks, and it combines with my altered body chemistry to make a sickliness chronic, a constant annoyance of nausea like a slimy seaweed clinging to the surface of the sea. Back in the city, I go to see the film, *Il Postino,* partly to take my mind off things. In this story of Pablo Neruda's friendship with a simple island postman, I am moved by the power of art to influence both politics and erotic love, by the links among all three. The politics are communist in the simplest sense, a love of ordinary people, which the film connects to a sensuous passion, to the natural world, and to poetry. I am trying as much as possible to focus on art, my own and that of others, believing, like the postman, in its mysterious erotic power to redeem.

Four doctors — two oncologists, my surgeon, and my own internist whom I trust as a friend — advised me to undergo chemotherapy, although my case, with a 2-centimeter tumor, was right on the borderline. There were estrogen receptors to measure, slow-growing and fast-growing tumors to distinguish, implications of being post- or premenopausal: conditions that have been rendered dangerously ambiguous by the prevalence of estrogen replacement therapy, a regimen of hormones I was on for over ten years. There are various chemicals in different chemotherapies to consider; some cause hair to fall out, some do not. Although the studies are not yet definitive, current practice recommends chemotherapy for everyone of a certain age, except those with the tiniest of tumors, and so I decide to submit to the business of poisoning myself in hopes of killing off dangerous, ravenous cells.

Oncologists seem to feel that in their relations with patients they have to choose between falsely optimistic cheer that amounts to denial, or ruthless verbal attack. The first oncologist I consulted looked me straight in the eye and said: "This is a systemic disease. The treatment is dangerous and difficult. You will immediately lose all your hair. Don't let anyone tell you it will be easy." She then recommended a course of chemotherapy of the harshest kind and followed up by undermining my internist, a man whom she knew well and the only medical person in whom I had complete confidence. When I sought a second opinion, at first I liked the seemingly more easygoing doctor and his "chemotherapy specialist" assistant and felt encouraged by their assurances. This doctor recommended a less toxic course of treatment. My blood count would probably remain at low normal, my hair would not fall out ("maybe get a little thinner, but you have nice, thick hair, you can afford to lose some"), and although I might get "a little sick," I would probably be fine. Perhaps such reassurances enabled me to wake up one morning and, accompanied by my sister who actually held me in her arms as the subway lurched downtown, go to the oncology unit for the first time. But as the months wore on, I came to see in this attitude a denial of reality, even a deception by the medical people, because to be reassured that one was not in imminent danger of dying seemed to mean that no talk of suffering or fear was acceptable at all.

Before every treatment, I experienced almost uncontrollable anxiety. Although there was no pain involved in the event itself, and I could sit up in a bright room with the door opened, I felt trapped and imprisoned during the entire hour I was attached to the IV, and the feeling of threatening panic continued until I was back at home. I have often wondered since then why chemo-therapy was so much more frightening to me than surgery or radiation. Perhaps it was the sight of the liquid dripping into my vein, its seeping, nauseating, unstoppable penetration; or the knowledge that this form of treatment is so full of uncertainty and potential danger; or the subtle and yet dramatic physical changes one sees and feels in the body and face—the eyes cloud, the skin seems to pale, hair texture alters even if it doesn't fall out. I know I felt completely out of control of my own physical boundaries, and the experience of nausea opened trapdoors to deeper, more primal feelings of disgust. The source of the nausea was inside my body, and became entangled with old feelings of shame. During the months of chemotherapy, I was aware of a vague, chronic sense of humiliation. I was reminded of the dead, disintegrating bodies of my dream.

After the first treatment, I was so relieved to be back home I actually felt joyful despite the weakness and queasiness I experienced for several days. After the second I engaged in a mad rush of physical activity, trying to copy a young Israeli woman who was my "treatment partner," and whose energy and optimism were both a standard and inspiration to me.

In the hospital, waiting to be called in for the third treatment, I try not to look closely at the ill-looking, sometimes emaciated, often hairless fellow patients. I want to feel stoical, self-contained, and these capacities require that I also feel distanced and different from them.

Today when I enter the small treatment room, another woman is already there, attached to her IV. She has dyed blond hair, good long legs, a body that looks about forty beneath a face that looks about sixty-five. Inserted into her chest is a tube that receives the IV through which her weekly chemotherapy drips, treating her lung cancer. With tears in her eyes and the sudden intimacy I've become used to with treatment partners, she tells me how she hates and fears these weekly treatments, how she can't sleep at night for fear. Just then, the nurse, the "chemotherapy specialist," enters, a sweet but distracted woman who once inserted the needle into my right arm, the arm that has lost its lymph nodes and is never supposed to be pricked with a needle, nor even squeezed by a blood pressure monitor. Then, obviously afraid of getting in trouble, she blamed me because I had held out the wrong arm, and indeed it was my fault as much as hers. I had been advised by doctors and books since the beginning to take charge of my own illness. I knew I was never supposed to be treated in that arm. But in my anxious state, I didn't realize it until I tried to pick up my pen to write in my journal and realized I couldn't write my way through the threatening forty-five minutes, as I often did, because my right arm was attached to a needle, a long tube, and an I V.

Now, she tells the other woman that she is bringing in a new patient who will need the same implanted tube, the same weekly chemotherapy. "But we don't want to scare her," she whispers like a conspiratorial schoolgirl, "so keep your mouth shut." The new patient, who is young and frightened and who has recently had a mastectomy, is brought into the room. My partner obeys orders, perhaps believing it is kinder to lie than to terrify, and says cheerfully, "Here, have a look. See? It's nothing really." Nurse and doctor echo the mood, smiling, patting, and chattering as if we are at a party. My somber expression and tone annoy them more and more as the weeks go by, as do my questions about physical reactions that depart from their predictions. "Well, it shouldn't happen," they will say when I describe days of weakness. "Are you back at work?"—implying that I am sitting around thinking about my illness too much, and that is why I am weak and have stomach pain. "I'm a writer," I mumble, hoping they will misunderstand or ignore me, because I certainly can't explain that I am writing about my illness, rushing home after every treatment to make copious notes. "It's not so bad, is it?" I am asked repeatedly, and I am expected to answer optimistically, cheerfully. Not to do so makes me feel like a failure, purposely complaining, a bad girl, and so, like my partner, I keep my mouth shut, having learned long ago how few people can understand the emotional intensity I live with all the time, which I try to manage but can never deny. If the expression of fear and pain to a receptive, sympathetic ear is an aspect of healing, as I believe is true, these rooms are not the place to engage in such unpleasantness. I learn to wait for visits to my therapist, or to my internist, a rare doctor who is afraid neither of pain nor of the fact that he cannot always "cure" it, yet might assuage it by listening to the narrative of another's experience with its often strangely familiar detail.

In this office, the destruction of possible cancer cells is accomplished with technical efficiency based on statistical analysis. I am given computer printouts that indicate the relative normalcy of my white blood count. I am given Tylenol to lessen the headaches caused by the antinausea drug. When the plastic bag of chemicals is empty and the needle removed from my hand, I am always quite dizzy, but leaning on the arm of Douglas whom, I am scolded by the doctors, I should not really need to accompany me anymore, I can return home. In terms of emotional isolation, I feel very much as I did when I was pregnant and had my first child. In both experiences, all the books, doctors, and even some of the women I tried to talk to assured me of how easy it all was, and so, because it was not only difficult but often overwhelming for me, I felt alone, weaker than they were, a failure in ways as familiar and almost as old as my life. "You'll adjust," I was told by numerous people seeking to help me when I was a child and my mother disappeared for good. I did, if adjusting means one doesn't keep on crying every day. But feelings remain large in me, needing recounting, rephrasing, revising as the years go by.

My partner raises her eyebrows at me after the new patient leaves the room, her cynical smile belied by the tears filling her eyes. "I didn't pay attention to the signs of my colon cancer," she tells me, "so it went to my lung, and now I'm paying the price." Treacherously, I count off our differences, distancing myself from her with notches of relative well-being. But when I look into her eyes I see what I don't want to see. I see that this woman knows more of what I am feeling than Douglas, or my children, or my friends. She knows because she has cancer, and so I know that I have had cancer, as my mother had cancer. She, too, is suddenly real to me. I have counted on our differences for too many years to know how to get along without them, that dark definitive line I first tried with all my might to cross, then growing away from her, older and older, was glad to see gathering distance behind me. But I see her now, lying in a dark room—young, in pain, and afraid—her legs too weakened to uphold her body when she gets out of bed to respond to her child's cry. I see her room, dark and eerie, the white of her sheets glowing slightly in the night. Then I see the room in the light of day, only my father's room now, her bed, her clothing, her body all gone. I can almost remember her voice, almost hear her actual scream before I back away quickly out the door and into the hall.

In the treatment room, staring at the open doorway, I am still attached to the iv that leaks its final drops into my vein. I turn back to my partner and reach out to touch her hand.

That night, I dream I am swimming in a dark, warm lake. Although I cannot lift my right arm to swim as well as I once could, I am making progress through the thick waters, and in the slow, effortful movement, I am soothed.

Three days later, the heat wave breaks. The sky is gray. Wind whips the clean light curtains in and out of the open window in my living room. I walk out onto my small terrace feeling a cool, soft rain on my face and bare feet. Newly planted flowers blow in the wind. I breathe deeply, noting the absence of nausea. A weird agitation I always feel for the first two days after the treatment is gone. I can be still, just feeling the wind, the rain.

And what of Ruthie's description of me as being so desperately attached to love? My grief at losing my mother is relived with each separation from my children; the passion I once felt for her has been replaced by an attachment to them so central to my being I try to hide the extremity of my own need and pretend to a freer love, more spacious and pure. The early confluence of extraordinary and even ordinary anger with guilt and punishment will haunt me as long as I live, each time I love deeply and fear abandonment, or am not loved in return. I have understood the indisputable truth of these sentences for some time. But now I am after another distinction, to unlock in myself a confusion between intensity of feeling and extremity of fear. The second, I hope, can be analyzed and perhaps diminished by retelling and renaming past losses, breaking the tie that reforms repeatedly in me between old threats and new, opening a wide chasm filled with murky rushing waters of past, never fully evaporated sorrow. The first, I am trying to see in a new way, to be brave enough to face the notion that the power of my love and need for love is neither crazy nor bad, even when reciprocation is uneven, or return denied.

Once again, I am about ten years old, a monitor at the school door. I wanted to go down on my knees, crawl on my belly, pound the concrete with my fists and beg that woman to be my mother. But she must have seen the desperation in my eyes, perhaps she was frightened of me, or thought me pitiful, when she began leaving her child farther down the block. When I see myself staring and longing, I feel both shame and anger and I try to mute the sound of my anguish by imagining the replacements I found. I am too far away to see the details of the mother's embrace, but I begin to whisper to myself about the precise way her mouth grazes the boy's cheek, her fingers moving through his hair, down to his forehead where she smooths his eyebrows with her thumb. I keep watching, turning away from my monitoring duties, even at that distance trying to feel the love, to steal it and let it fill the emptiness inside me with images and words.

Intimacy Itself

What art was there, known to love or cunning, by which one pressed through into those secret chambers? What device for becoming, like waters poured into one jar, inextricably the same, one with the object one adored? Could the body achieve, or the mind, subtly mingling in the intricate passages of the brain? or the heart? Could loving, as people called it, make her and Mrs. Ramsay one? for it was not knowledge but unity that she desired, not inscriptions on tablets, nothing that could be written in any language known to men, but intimacy itself, which is knowledge, she had thought, leaning her head on Mrs. Ramsay's knee.
—Virginia Woolf, *To the Lighthouse*

I am sitting in Aaron's room. Throughout this intense winter, nearly every Friday, the day of my session, there is a storm outside. I hear the wind whipping down the street, rattling the windows as I talk to this man I have known less than a year, yet who has become more intimately aware of my interior life than anyone I know or love. The afternoon turns dark early because of the storms, the shadowy light gives a gray cast to the muted colors of the room, to his white or light blue shirt and gray pants, to his pale skin and aging face. I love the storms—the sound of them outside and walking through them the ten blocks from my apartment. No mask of anger or anxiety covers the more difficult emotions. My sorrow is sharp and precise. It is not threatening. Like the storm, it is already there.

I came here for the first time only two weeks after my breast surgery. Within three months I came to trust Aaron, within six months to love him. It is a strange word to use for someone you hardly know, whose knowledge of you is only of your innermost thoughts, who is not familiar with how you talk about ordinary things, how you cook or walk down the street, or sleep or eat. It is a distillation of love, perhaps, bringing love down to some essential component. Just as, in this narrative, I am trying to create a distillation of all the raw and chaotic feeling I have experienced in the past few years; not simply to describe desolation or anger, but to find some essential reality beneath them both.

This winter I enjoy the immense luxury of a sabbatical from my teaching job. I focus my life on writing this narrative as if it were a heavy porous log I cling to after the ship has long sunk and disappeared beneath dark waves. One or two hours a week I confess the details of my interior life not only to the pages of my journal, but to another human being. I sought help in a kind of panic that life was slipping away from me, that in some mysterious way two years of despair had worn down my immune system and helped give me breast cancer. This may not be true, of course. Nevertheless, I proceed with my three-part effort as if it were. I reread old journals, then rewrite my stories hoping to glimpse meaning or order through an altered perspective. I search for connections among old and recent sorrows, and for words resonant enough to stand for the many parts that remain untold. Once a week, I tell my stories to Aaron. I fight off shame, reticence, fear, embarrassment, modesty, faintness of heart, and lack of faith. Thoughts must be caught and faced and said out loud, and they must be said to another person, to him. He stares back at me with enormous intensity. He speaks of his associations, makes interpretations, at times reveals emotional reactions of his own. He keeps well within the boundaries of therapeutic dialogue and psychoanalytic practice, but the emotion is real. I am counting on that. It is only in the authenticity of his emotion that I am brave enough to relive the stories I believe I must relive in order to recover my health, to face the loneliness at the center of my life.

Now, reading back to the daily notes I made during the six weeks of radiation treatments, I come upon a defining image whose meaning unravels infinitely, it seems. I am lying on the table under the radiation machine, before the actual treatment begins. They turn out the lights in order to adjust the rays, which are visible only in the dark. While it is dark, my breast is reflected in the lens above me. I see a silhouette of my breast behind the computerized red lines moving and jumping across the lens. It is *the breast*, as the doctors called it, and it, the breast, is reflected in the lens so it can be shot through with perfectly aimed radiation. But it is my breast, and I want to reach out for the reflection, trace the line of the curve — its delicate, singular, unique grace, the curve so familiar to me, like the print of a painting you have had for years on your wall and you come upon it unexpectedly in a museum and you think — what is it doing here? Or, like a beloved piece of music building toward a particular series of notes you wait for and wait for, then soar with as the perfectly known melody is found again. Throughout the weeks of radiation, this view of my breast is so painful I have to close my eyes against the dark reflection until, the point of the machine perfectly in place, my arm raised above my head, my body slightly off center so that my right breast is raised toward the machine, they turn on the lights again, the reflection disappears, and I am surrounded by bright, stark emptiness. Everyone leaves the room. A loud, screeching noise begins, indicating radiation is in progress. Then loneliness is a river I am swept down, rushing into my past, which grows clearer and clearer as I move. Alongside that river is another place that scares me much more than loneliness — my anger, my rage. As long as the two remain parallel, I can keep a safe distance between them, but then they converge, water soaking land, land filling water, until thick mud is all there is. I move through it, my ankles and calves held fast in the dirt, which hardens like clay. Just below my anger, which these weeks can rise instantaneously like a sudden volcano spewing forth ash beyond my control, is always the image of my breast, its graceful silhouette, and the image calms my anger even as it floods me with remembered grief.

It is a year before, the early spring of 1994 and Douglas's brother Simeon is dying of A I D S. He has been struggling against an intestinal virus for five months, but he has lost the battle and the virus has gone to his brain. In a hospital in San Francisco, he lies in a coma from which no one expects him to awaken. His mother, Lois, has been with him for months, and now his remaining brother, his sister, Sherrill, his niece Tiffani, Khary, and I fly to San Francisco where Adam will join us. It is a strange kind of appointment. We are going to accompany Simeon to his death, to obey his clearly stated wish that we all be there when he dies.

At the airport, we are picked up by Gabriel and Pete, Simeon's friends with whom we will become temporarily, yet profoundly, intimate over the coming days. They drive us to the hospital where Lois is utterly distraught, walking the halls in her plaid nightshirt, having just received the worst news. Douglas looks more upset than I have seen him in years, and remains a long time in the privacy of the room with Simeon, holding his brother's hands, whispering to him on the chance he might be able to hear. And then, we take him home to die.

Like many others, I had fallen in love with Lois when I met her twenty-five years before. She taught me a great deal about African American life and culture, explaining generously to her white daughter-in-law the intricate realities of racism and history most whites fail to understand. She guided me through experiences during Adam's and Khary's childhood I could not have managed nearly as well without her. I had written about her in my novels and memoirs, and she was a central support to me in the book I was writing about race. We both grew up as motherless daughters, and this has been a source of many commonalities between us. Dramatic, passionate, beautiful, even at seventy, she is a magnetic woman of many gifts. But disabling griefs over the past years — the loss of a husband, of her eldest son, now of her youngest — have shifted the balance between her magnetism and powerful love on one hand, her anger at life's injustice and fearful self-protection on the other. "I hope he knew we'd take care of you," she had said to me when my father died and I was twenty-seven, she forty-seven years old. She could not have imagined the tragedies ahead of her then, the patterns and intentions grief would revise. When I take her in my arms in the hospital corridor, she remains stiff, her arms at her sides. When I reach down to hold her hands, they remain fists as my fingers enclose them. During all the days of Simmie's dying, my grief and fear will be laced with anger — childish, unjust, selfish, passionate anger — an easier mask, like Lois's, for longing and love.

We settle Simeon in his bed in the sunroom, one side lined with beautiful windows looking out on a garden. In the adjoining room, the friends who will help us through the next eight days begin to gather. Anne, who seems like a sister during that long week, whose hair is a mixture of blond and gray like my own sister's hair. Irene, who organizes a system of food delivery from acquaintances and friends. Tom, who was Simeon's partner for so long he has become like a member of our family. Dan, whose wife, Lee, is expecting a baby any day who will be named Simeon if a boy. Gabriel, one of Simmie's oldest friends, is a gay man who flaunts his gayness, daring anyone to question his movements, his eye makeup, the mixture of extraordinary courage and grim humor that make up his history; he was a draft resister during the Vietnam War and spent several years in prison; he is a nurse who has helped dozens of his friends as they died of AIDS; he calls Simmie his sister, and postures around, making us laugh. I wonder how my son Khary will handle this gay male expressiveness, but by the end of the week there will be no question in anyone's mind. He and Gabriel will be comrades. They will confer about medications and plans. They will embrace at the bedside when Simeon dies. Pete, Simeon's ex-lover, young and vulnerable, is able to help in intense spurts, then leaves suddenly, as if he has to escape. Like me, he seems to feel Simeon is angry with him, and indeed, according to Lois, Simmie has been angry, and quite harsh. During one of his semiconscious states, he looks at Pete and says, "I don't want . . ." Pete responds, "You don't want me here?" and leaves in tears.

On the second day, I sit on Simeon's bed and try to talk to him. He raises his hands like a cat's paws and snarls at me. "Oh it's just some brain synapse out of whack," Dan says, trying to comfort me. "He's just playing, kidding around," says Lois, and Douglas agrees. But he knew I had grown angry with him over the years, and I am afraid, after that, to get too close to him until the very last day.

By the third day, I begin to experience severe stomach pains. The conflict between my hunger for this family's love and my self-condemnation for anger as the hunger remains unassuaged will result in an ulcer by the time I return to New York. As I move through the week, this conflict drives me. I am longing for Lois to take me in her arms, for Douglas to cry with me, to feel I am the sister in the family I've been part of for nearly three decades.

As far back as I can remember, the phrase "almost like a daughter" has haunted me. Offered with genuine love by a number of older, maternal women, I nevertheless could focus only on the "almost," and often withdrew from the relationship, protecting desire with distance, substituting anger for need. Here, in the family closer to me than any other apart from my own, I am "almost" like a daughter again. But I am aware of these echoes going backward in time only with the indefinite consciousness that precedes words. I know I desire something not to be had, something I feel selfish and guilty for desiring. I cannot find the language to describe the feelings because the feelings themselves still make me ashamed. I turn to the sink to wash the many dishes that pile up each day, to the telephone to keep track of the numerous calls, to the broom, the sorting of newspapers, the shopping for food and medical supplies.

Writing this part of the story, even now, two years later, I back off, fatigued, agitated. My neck is rigid, my shoulders ache. I see my breast on the dark lens, Simeon's eyes focused on his mother's face, my mother's face becoming less shadowy. Her eyes are closed as she lies on her deathbed in a darkened room. A nurse sits by her side. I am peering in from the doorway, wanting to run up to her, leap on her, wake her up, but I remain quiet as I have been told to do a hundred times. Although I intended to

write this in a linear time frame, trying to keep to a calendar of days, circularity quickly takes over, association
rather than chronology demanding expression in words.

During the eight-day vigil, Lois spends all her time
lying next to Simmie on his bed or caring for his physical
needs with the help of Douglas, Gabriel, and Anne. I cannot manage the physical care—cleaning him, attaching
the catheter—and I feel ashamed for this inability. I keep
a notebook of information: visitors, nursing schedules,
mortuary and hospice information, medications. I keep
up my determined, useful housework. I talk to the friends
about Simmie's wishes to be "helped toward death," trying to decide when we should begin to increase the morphine as the doctors have taught us to do "when the time
comes." I try to spare Lois and Douglas the specifics of
that decision, feeling it is the least I can do.

Every day or two, I return to my sister's house in Berkeley for some hours of respite from the dying, which is
unlocking memories hunched for years at the bottom of
my life. My mother's body, fragile and helpless, is continually before me, and I am a child again. Dust and white
bone fill my dreams at night. But I am also escaping Lois's
anger. Her perfect ministrations to her child are accompanied by—perhaps even kept in place by—anger with
others in the family, including me. She snaps harshly. She
turns her face and sucks her teeth in a familiar gesture of
disapproval. She lashes out.

To the doctors' amazement, Simeon wakes up on the
second day, emerging from the coma, and from then on
he moves between wake and sleep, clearly recognizing
his mother, his brother and sister, some of his friends. But
once when I am sitting near him, talking to him softly,
he asks, "Who are you?" Stunned, I return to the front
stoop and stare into the sun. Outsider longing to be taken

in—daughter-in-law, I silently berate myself for childish needs. There is useful work for me to do. I walk back inside and stand in the doorway staring into the sunroom. Lois and Douglas are washing Simmie in a tender collaboration. Douglas lifts the frail body of his brother while their mother changes the sheet.

On the second night, Adam, an actor, leaves us for his home in Los Angeles because of an important part we all decide Simmie would not want him to sacrifice. He sits on the bed whispering his own private goodbye to the uncle he loves, telling him he has to return to tape a new part on a television show. Simmie smiles, lifts his arm high and draws an arc in the air, as if to say, reach for the sky. Then, standing in the middle of the room, surrounded by people who are witnessing his grief and trying not to stare, Adam weeps a long time in Khary's arms.

The Castro district, where Simmie lived, is crowded with people and shops like the Lower East Side of Manhattan, and I walk the steep hills many times a day, buying diapers, mattress pads, other supplies, the material necessities of illness usually provided by hospitals. No institutional veil or protection exists for the dying at home, no anesthetizing of the process. You don't leave the patient for a few hours behind a closed door while the nurses attend to the details, adjust the body to its slow relinquishing of life. Biological systems don't always break down uniformly. One thing stops slowly, then another. It is often impossible to tell what remains of ordinary consciousness and what is already gone. Simmie lies in a room with no door, separated from the rest of the small apartment by an open archway. We are as close to dying as we can get without dying ourselves.

Simmie communicates with his eyes, and even with some language, which the doctors thought he had lost.

"There are five of you," he says once, looking at a group surrounding his bed. Once, he calls for Adam, then raises his lips to be kissed. He keeps insisting he be allowed to get up, and when Gabriel refuses to let him do so, he says, "Fuck you. I have to get my feet on the ground." Another night, he tells Lois that Sallie, her long-dead mother, is in the room.

Khary and Tiffani spend their days doing chores, holding Simmie's hands, rubbing his head, much less afraid than I am of the experience of dying. I am remembering all the conflict we had in recent years involving Simmie's extreme need for attention, his inability, at times, to pay attention to others who needed him. I was angry, then distant, resentful of how easily he made his own needs the center of his life. Then, when I lost track of my needs, he would come to me in a dream, symbolizing an admirable, creative self-involvement. When I began this narrative, I dreamed I was in an old basement where I discovered a manuscript I'd forgotten to complete, a treasure. The manuscript was buried among Simmie's books and files. During the week he is dying I feel too confused to face such ambivalence. I am afraid that I will prove inadequate to the tasks of care. Anne and Irene encourage me while we walk around the neighborhood or sit in the blessed hours of sun on Simeon's front steps. These two women, who were unknown to me the week before, who are still in certain ways strangers, give me the courage to continue with the death work by listening to my confessions of anger and love, reminding me of my place in the family, the need for the kind of emotional strength I can provide. My feelings are raw and ragged, but my actions are protective, my labor efficient and smooth. Like a well-trained orderly, I attend seriously to the cleaning up.

The circle encloses us: Anne, Irene, Tom, Gabriel, Dan,

Pete, Tommy, a very warm and talkative man who is an Italian from Philadelphia, and Frank, who has AIDS himself. All these men and women are living in a plague time. They have lost many of their friends. Some of them will soon die themselves.

Each day, we expect Simeon to die, so most nights we all sleep together on mattresses spread out across the entire floor. Lois sleeps with Simeon, holding her son in her arms.

The visiting nurse tells us Simmie is exceptionally strong and could go on for days, and he begins discussions with us about administering the morphine dose based on his need. Simeon made several of us promise not to prolong his life if the virus went to his brain, and emphasized that when that happened he wanted to go as quickly as possible. Khary and Tiffani urge us to begin, but they are too young to realize how dire a decision in terms of its psychological consequences this really is. I sit by myself on the stoop, for an hour just thinking, not allowing myself to write, afraid the words might become a story and I will lose track of the barest truth. I try to picture myself doing it, feeding him the liquid that will alleviate his pain but may also hasten his death. I feel I cannot, partly because of my own ambivalent feelings and conflicts with him. But I tell Gabriel and Anne that if they can do it, I will share equally in the decision. We agree that Douglas and Lois should not be involved since they have given their general consent, that Khary and Tiffani can advise but must not be included in actual medical decisions. Anne says we should wait, that Simeon is still awake too often and, she believes, is waiting for Dan's baby to be born.

We are called to the bedside three times before the final time, all the signs indicating imminent death, but then he rallies, opens his eyes, asks for food or drink. Each time, the wracking emotions of a last good-bye are followed by the realization that he is not yet gone. Once, he recovers enough to look through his photograph albums, his beloved mementos of his travels, the record of his life.

Again, he sees Sallie, his long-dead grandmother, standing with his brother Ricky, and his father, Frederick, at the foot of his bed. If they were there, imagine how confused and pleased he must have been, to see us all there around him, the living and the dead, himself the fragile bridge between life and death for the long week it took him to cross over.

On the last day, after about five o'clock, Anne and Gabriel begin increasing the doses of morphine. Simeon has not been conscious for a full day and seems different from before. The doctor has assured us he is moving through his last hours. The day before, Dan's wife gave birth to their son, Simeon. Simmie had been told and seemed to understand. He had been shown photographs of the baby.

When night was falling and we'd been counting breaths and giving morphine for hours, Dan tells us that several weeks before a voice had come to him in a dream and said: It will be 3-18. His son, Simeon, had been born the night before, on March 10 at an hour that bore no relation to the numbers 3-18, so instead of going home, Dan is sitting out the night with the rest of us, at least until 3:30 A.M., he says.

We take turns sitting on the bed, counting breaths, two a minute. Still a fairly strong pulse. We wait. At 11 P.M., a night nurse arrives and says the end is near.

Khary sits beside him for hours, holding his hand, stroking his forehead. I am afraid he will suffer later, but he is determined to remain close, in part, I think, because

Douglas is keeping so fierce a distance. Nor can I sit for hours watching every moment of the dying. But wherever we are in the apartment, we can hear the increasingly loud and labored breathing, not a "death rattle," more like boulders rolling across the land, or a large drum. Douglas begins to fall asleep, which causes Khary to become upset and I keep waking him, but then seeing the stress in his eyes, the tightness of his jaw, that he cannot bear this deathwatch, I suggest that he lie down in the other room, where his sister has already retreated, and he falls asleep immediately. Tiffani has gone outside to stand in the night air, and I tell Khary I think she needs him. He goes out and stands on the stoop with her. I wrap them both in one large, red blanket so they look like a homeless couple, two utterly beautiful, lost beings in the night.

At about midnight, several of us are standing outside, and Dan tells us again about his dream. Khary and I go to a corner store to buy ice cream pops, which everyone grabs and devours. I so wish Adam were with us, for his strength and humor, and because we are all so profoundly cemented by this experience I fear we will never be able to fully describe.

For hours, those two breaths a minute come. We eat and drink and laugh at ourselves for all the eating. Then the laughter disappears in an instant, like a note with no echo, the sound completely gone. Some drift back to the bed, others to chairs. I go outside for long periods to escape the terrible sound of the breaths. I remember Charlotte Brontë's descriptions of her beloved sister Emily's death, the interminable hours of thinking the end is coming any minute, the medications and herbs used to "ease the way," the sound of the painful struggle for breath as the lungs fill with liquid. She sat in the kitchen waiting for her third sister to die, and she felt her lifelong loneliness surround

her, familiar in its dampness, its pungent smell. The loneliness was both destiny and curse, partner to "a sense of
unworthiness," she called it, "never to be erased." * Shadows cross and recross in the dark, sounds coming from
far away, anger coming from far away, love even farther
back, a nearly imperceptible shape, as narrow as a line.

My teeth begin to ache as I write, a familiar sign of
powerlessness in myself. I felt powerless in those last
moments, not only in the human battle with death but in
my own capacity to love as generously as I would have
wished. Just as I was expressing my pent-up anger to
Irene, the nurse rushed over and said Simmie had died.
There was a sudden silence. No breathing. He seemed
peaceful, his face expressionless, blank, or pure, his body
only flesh, the spirit gone. It was exactly 3:18 A.M. Dan's
dream undid my belief in linear time, my faith in the
orderly chronology of human stories. I smelled the acrid
loneliness, then it was washed away leaving a blinding
emptiness behind. I felt shocked, exactly as if we hadn't
been waiting for seven, almost eight days, ashamed of
my angry thoughts at the very moment of his death. As if
I had been given the chance to do it over, better this time,
as an adult, and had failed again. I wanted to cry in Lois's
arms, to hold Douglas while he cried, to fill the middle of
just one silent night with my own cries. But I had no tears.
Coldness kept my neck stiff, my angry fists at my sides.

I woke Douglas and called Tiffani and Khary inside
where we gathered around the bed one last time. Everyone embraced everyone else, like at New Year's Eve. Lois
knelt by the body and sobbed, "I cannot live without
you," as if there were one last moment when he might
still hear. Tiffani lifted her up and finally, after everyone

*Helene Moglen, *Charlotte Brontë: The Self Conceived* (New
York: Norton, 1976).

else had stepped away, she and Douglas, her last remaining son, embraced.

We covered Simeon, closed his eyes. Lois and Sherrill retreated to the one bedroom behind a closed door. Somewhat madly, Dan, Irene, Douglas, and I cleaned the kitchen. Anne drove Tiffani and Khary back to Berkeley while we waited for the undertaker. When he came, Douglas and I joined Lois and Sherrill in the bedroom so we wouldn't have to witness the final leaving. I sat on the floor, laid my head down on the bed and in a second fell asleep. In a few minutes I was awake again, listening to the sounds of the body being taken away.

When we emerged, all was changed, the bed folded back into the couch, the room empty of people and chairs. Lois insisted all she wanted was to be left alone to go to sleep. Douglas and I drove back to Berkeley in the dawn.

A month after Simeon's death, we gather in San Francisco again for a memorial. I rise to speak to the large crowd, but I keep my eyes on Khary, Adam, and Tiffani. I speak to them about the family, remembering their grandfather Frederick, Tiffani's father, Ricky, now Simeon joining the dead. The tears I could not shed at his bedside are plentiful now. I am speaking through sobs but I push on, naming the ways I have belonged to them all, seeing the ways I never will.

Back East, when I record the story of those days, I am sitting on the steps of a house near the Long Island Sound. I raise my face to the sun, which is strong despite a heavy snowfall the previous night. As I complete the task of record keeping, listening to the sound of the gentle waves, I think of Dan's prophetic dream and I feel my father near me, for a moment perhaps even my mother. A sense of belonging somewhere, to someone, grazes me, the edge of memory calling the name of my need. But now it is gone, replaced again by loneliness; the memory of my mother's fragile wrists resting on smooth, white sheets; the bones of Simmie's skull, his skeletal thighs; the curve of my breast beneath the radiation machine; the very loneliness that leads me back to the stories I am trying to knit together with borders of words.

The first stage of the six weeks of radiation is something called a Simulation, a process several hours long that readies the body for treatment. I lie on a table, one arm raised above me, while a mold is made around my head and shoulders. I am filmed, measured with wires and rods. Five small marks are tattooed in a circle around my right breast to frame the space within which the radiation will occur. For nearly an hour I lie on a table with one breast exposed, six or seven doctors and technicians moving around me, filming, measuring. Large machines loom over me, seem as if they might drop any minute, crushing me. My back aches terribly after a half hour, but I am obedient and do not move. Sorrow flows over the future in an infinite wash. Delineation disappears. Time seems horribly amorphous, without normal contours, and to contain the panic this causes I whisper, *August, September, six weeks, five days a week plus two, thirty-two days.*

It is August 6, Hiroshima Day. The papers are filled with old photographs of people burning alive, dying in large numbers from radiation. Daily, there is news of a Republican congress that strips the poor of all supports, blaming the weakest among us for their inability to survive heroically against the greatest odds. The Unabomber prints his mad declaration in major newspapers, and threaded through his homicidal, power-hungry, racist and sexist madness is a quite sane fear of technology, a critique of the very idea of progress. If technology is curing my cancer, I have also been warned that it could create new cancers, cause damage to other organs as the breast is cured. I feel insane, like the Unabomber terrified of the world. I am filled with rage at politicians who are trying to destroy ordinary people and increase extraordinary corporate profits. I weep at the sight of old, charred bodies in Japan. Once I constructed a dry, internal distance to protect me from feelings always too raw, desires too naked. Now, with the swiftness of lightning in a storm, that distance is crossed by any suffering I see. Inside, I am moist, storm-threatened. I am not heroic. I cry each day before my treatment, and during the treatment I have to work hard not to sob out loud.

Summer heat swells my feet and fingers, which need repeated immersion in ice cold water when I am home. At night I drape cool rags across my forehead and chest. Even in air-conditioned rooms, I cannot stop sweating. During the day, I clean house, oil wooden floors, plant and sweep the terrace, reorder shelves, and wash the refrigerator, controlling what I can.

Some days, lying on the radiation table, I try to think of the Wellfleet Bay I love, but I begin to cry from the contrast, and these tears lead immediately to tears of longing for Adam. I think about his great bravery, his more difficult — because it is daily and lifelong — disease of diabetes. With the tears, my body begins to move, so I decide to block out all feeling, concentrate on the radio music being piped in, the white walls around me, the slightly stained ceiling above.

On many days, I wait forty-five minutes to be called in, growing more and more agitated as the minutes pass. Other patients recount their stories to each other, their voices threatening to permeate the walls I have erected around me as I stare into my journal or book. One day, a woman begins to talk to me. "I am out of my mind with fear" she says, and shows me the burn on her breast after three weeks, a large area of nearly blue black on dark brown skin. I have been warned of burns but have not imagined them so definitively. A very ill-looking South American man is accompanied by several members of his family. His throat is bandaged, his face terribly swollen, his eyes swollen too, and bloodshot, from weeping or disease. Every so often, he has to vomit, and a woman places a steel tray under his chin. I close my book and rush into the hallway, pace, turn my back, breathe.

In the interior waiting room I change out of my shirt and into a cotton gown. Raisa, a new technician, a woman of about twenty, is clearly upset by my crying, and I try to stop for her, but although I can contain the sound, water keeps flowing out of my eyes, down my cheeks, over my chin, onto my throat. I am amazed that I have so many tears, remembering myself at Simeon's deathbed, eyes as dry as ice.

Jamar, a warm, competent young man who is the head technician, asks me what is wrong. I try to explain that not knowing what is about to happen to me is terrifying, that I cannot bear the other patients talking in the waiting room. I tell him that I listen to their tales of illness with my eyes cast down, writing ceaselessly so no one will talk directly to me, give me the weight of their stories. I tell him there is an old man who walks around in a diaper, no robe covering him, as if he has given up the struggle for dignity. There is a woman prisoner with long, gray matted hair and a pockmarked face, whose legs are in irons and who comes in each morning accompanied by two women guards. When I don't hear the stories, or overhear them, I imagine them, or make them up. I take them in and they become me, and I need all my strength to feel in control of my own story, to get through this ordeal. I tell Jamar all this, finally breaking into sobs, and I apologize, tell him he is probably too young to understand. "I am not that young," he says, offended, "I am thirty years old, and I do understand." From that moment on, he gives me detailed coming attractions each day when I leave of what to expect the next day. As soon as he sees me in the waiting room, he ushers me into a quieter hallway where I can pace or sit alone until it is my turn. I feel very selfish compared to those who can talk and listen for hours. But in the following weeks, two or three other people will confess to me the hardest part for them, too, is waiting with the other patients, listening to the terrible stories. So we are a group of a sort, not really selfish, only permeable.

One day as I wait, I see Dr. C., the radiation oncologist. I ask her if there is any danger to overlapping the radiation with chemotherapy, as they are doing in my case. "When both are given together there is almost always a worse burning of the breast accompanied by shooting pains, but none of it is anything to worry about," she informs me crisply. "How much pain?" I ask, trying to picture it, give it dimension and so contain my fear. "Just some discomfort," she responds impatiently. I am being a bad patient again by refusing to see this is all something that can easily be managed with a stiff upper lip. "Well then," I ask, "why don't they halt the chemotherapy while I am in radiation?" And right there, in the waiting room, she begins to shout at me: "We are dealing with your longevity here. Do you want to compromise your longevity?!"

I meet a young woman with a black cross on her throat

marking the place where they direct the ray. As I walk toward her, she tells me she has just finished her treatments, and she falls into my arms. We remain that way, rocking each other, strangers who will never see each other again. The next day, when I go into the bathroom to get dressed, I see the same black cross on my chest. I try to get it off with water, but it seems indelible, and I am filled with anxiety about what it means. I ask the attendant, and he tells me with a stunning, callous smile that it is nothing, only a mark for their convenience. No reason, he repeats. Comes off with an alcohol swab. When I describe the anxiety of finding it and the symbolic meaning of a black cross, he apologizes for their insensitivity and promises that from now on he will give people the swabs in advance.

Each day, I lie back on the table, find my place within the blue head and shoulder mold, raise my arm to its awkward position, lift my legs over the pillow they provide for some comfort and begin to cry. I lie perfectly still under the machine. In the dark, I close my eyes so I will not see the reflection of my breast. Then, the light on again, the sustained loud screeching noise, which at first intensified my fear by giving sound to the violence being done to my body, is familiar by now, even slightly comforting, something to count against. Between forty-five and fifty-seven seconds, then Jamar and Raisa return, remove the slides, push the machine to the side, give me a hand to sit up and I am through.

One day after the treatment, I meet my friend Sally for lunch. In a small, book-lined restaurant where we munch on salads and sip diet Cokes, I begin to cry again, for the first time with someone other than the technicians and Douglas. Sally has remained completely focused on me through months of illness, consistently attentive, willing to walk me to the radiation unit in the depths of the basement of the hospital, wait for me there, or meet me afterward, interrupting her own work for an elegant or ordinary lunch. She looks into my eyes steadily. There is no sense of discomfort in her gaze. She will listen as long as I can talk. She is giving me just the thing I need most and cannot ask for. In the attentive warmth of her friendship, I feel its opposite, the hot rage and grief I must have felt as a child slinking around doorways, trying to be quiet while my mother died. My father, aunts, and grandmother must have been too stunned or frightened or selfish to listen to children's cries, which were unassuageable anyway, and might as well be silenced as encouraged. Pieces slide together slowly, right beneath the surface. I try to hold Lois but her grief is too immense for comfort. Her anger ignites mine. It is stiffening. She cannot hold me back.

A young woman across from me in the waiting room reads her Bible and quietly prays out loud. I write a calendar of dates in my journal: Next week I will see a close friend who is visiting from Israel. The week after that, Adam is coming home. By then, it will be nearly September and I will have just two more weeks to go. I feel stronger when I write these notes, and the strength lasts through the treatment and on the walk back across town. But on the subway going home, I sit next to a woman who is holding her child. He is about four or five years old. Dangerously, I notice the fragility of his arms wrapped around her neck, their graceful curving lines. Then I remember the delicacy of Adam's arms, of Khary's, when they were that age, their arms encircling my shoulders, my neck. I see the half-moon curve of a child's thigh in a Kathe Kollwitz drawing. And I see the silhouette of my breast on the screen. The beautiful shape, the delicate roundness of the curve, the dark oval crossed by computerized red lines, identifying the target for the rays.

As the days and weeks go on and my skin begins to burn and scale, my emotions grow large, devouring distance and control. Anxiety after only a few moments of waiting. A level of exhaustion I could not have imagined. Panic threatens each morning as I get ready to go downtown to the hospital. I begin to see I will have to ask for more help, for Douglas or Khary or Sally to accompany me more often.

One weekend, I return to the grassy beach in Long Island and take a long walk through the shallow sound. Softly, water moves against my body, caressing my breast and my right arm which is still sore from the surgical removal of lymph nodes. I walk out where it is deeper. I lie down. Fluid and at peace, I let my head sink beneath the water and taste the salt on my lips and tongue. Then at night I hurt my arm slightly when lifting a window, and the small pain opens the flood gates. I cry uncontrollably. I cannot be quieted. I long for my father to hold me, standing by my bed, which I stand on, so that our shoulders are the same height, to hear him say, Go on, cry, *Ketseleh*, cry it out. I long to feel his mouth against my hair as his cries rise to match mine until we are both calling her, holding onto each other, patting each others' backs while he smooths my hair, the flood of our tears intermingling on my cheeks, and I taste the salty water in my mouth.

Only in the last two weeks do I begin to relax into a slightly thicker skin, partly because the end is in sight, partly because I have become friends with Raisa and Jamar, which eases the surface loneliness. The summer itself, which loomed so monstrously in May and June, a huge giant of time lying still and unmovable before me, is nearing its end. After the summer, only two weeks of radiation and two more chemotherapy treatments will be left to go.

In the unit, people reach their last day and emerge with paper diplomas. An emaciated blond woman who must be over sixty looks like a blushing girl when she announces her "graduation," and her face lights up the room. I tell Jamar that while I don't want to hurt anyone's feelings, I do not want a photocopied diploma when I leave, that to me it feels like a trivialization of all I have been through. He reacts with his usual kindness, now made more precious by his growing knowledge of me. "I didn't think you would," he says, smiling. I realize, with some astonishment, that when I am finished I will miss these intelligent young medical workers whose capacity for sympathy and fearlessness in the face of suffering is so much greater than the doctors whom they serve. I almost begin to feel at home. Instead of leaving my bra and shirt in a locker, I take them into the treatment room with me now and quickly put them on when I climb off the table, so I can walk swiftly back through the rooms and onto the street.

In the last week, a new dark-haired young woman appears. She looks no older than twenty-one or two, and like me she is quiet, always reading her book. One morning she waits and waits, but she is not called. The receptionist, in her usual oblivious, haughty mood, makes no mention of it. The South American man is sick again, and begins to vomit. The young woman and I rush to the inner waiting room to escape. I ask if she has been waiting long, and she responds, yes, for over an hour. Soon, a nurse with a strong New York accent, who has told me she writes "stawrries and po-ems," a kind woman who welcomes me into back rooms to wait when she sees my "nerves," comes into the room. But she motions to me that it is my turn. I tell her the young woman has been waiting much longer than I have. She rushes off to investigate, finds they have made a mistake, did not know she was there, and thanking me, they take her first. I will have to wait another twenty minutes, but I feel strong, maternal, adequate to the task at hand.

When I was a child the word *mother* was precious to me. I hung onto it like the torn edge of a shredded blanket a child carries around as talisman, omen, secret good luck charm. I felt paralyzed with envy when I heard other children saying Mommy, or Mom (with casual entitlement) or Mother. I'd stand still, watching, trying to match the sound of the lost word with emotions the child speaking must have been feeling. I'd have to stand very still to focus my energy, to will the tears to remain inside, not to move into my throat and become a scream.

For years when I spoke of my mother, I would never call her Mother, certainly not Mom, or Mommy, but Tullah, her name. I tried to face the reality that if *mother* signals the deepest possible intimacy or at least familiarity, I had no mother at all, and when I married Douglas I knew immediately that I would call his mother by her name. We would be friends, I said, long practiced in resisting illusions about substitutes, maintaining a cold, uncompromising eye on the truth. Only after I had breast cancer did I begin, for the first time since childhood, to unearth the impossible desire for someone, anyone, to take her place. During the long months of treatment, I wanted no one more than a mother. I would not say *my mother*, because I still had only the barest recollection of her and did not focus my yearning on her particular face. Like many sons and daughters who are themselves middle-aged, even those with living mothers, when I yearned for a mother it was the mother of my dreams.

During my first few sessions with Aaron, after I had surgery but had still not fully comprehended that I'd actually had cancer, I told him of my mother and the old fear that she and I were somehow the same person, that in order to overcome the deadly identification I had to banish her. He said, "Well, you are not her, but you are her daughter." The simplicity of his statement stunned me. Both things could be true at once then, an ordinary reality I hadn't considered for many years. It would take eight more months before I could remember loving her, the searing pain when I lost her forever, before I could reclaim her from her sisters, her mother, my father, all the voices who insisted she was perfectly magnificent and therefore couldn't be mine.

Raisa asks me if I am feeling better, as I am crying less. I say becoming attached to her and Jamar has helped. She responds, "Yes, that's the trouble with this job. You get attached to people and then they disappear; but I understand you, Ms. Lazarre," she tells me. "My boyfriend is just like you. Really sensitive. A lot on his mind." This is one of the few times I am comfortable being called Ms. Lazarre when I am using the other person's first name. With building workers, my students, my children's friends, and certainly with doctors when I am on the other side, I hate the hierarchy of respect this inequality of naming often represents. But here, it is literally a saving grace. Like a dancer's movement, I feel my back straighten, my face raised as if to receive a blessing from the sky. I put my arm around Raisa for a moment to thank her, place my open palm against her head, feeling the heavy weight of her thick, soft, dark brown curls.

By the last week, a deep purple line extends under my breast, across the incision under my arm. Otherwise, everything is dark red, looking burnt, which is exactly what it is. I am unable to relax or sleep when I am home, afraid of relinquishing my vigilance. The image of my mother comes to me frequently now. Sometimes her face, staring up at the ceiling as she lies in bed knowing she is going to die. Sometimes, the face in her photograph, which has remained for years buried in a drawer, although all our other ancestors are framed and cover one narrow wall, a tribute to memory. Sometimes I imagine her bones, what must be left of her body after forty-five years. They lie in the shape of a woman, but they have fallen apart, no longer attached to each other by the connection of flesh. They remind me of my own skeleton as I saw it depicted on a large computer screen the day I had a bone scan. I keep a vigil. Otherwise everything, the bones, the unattached memories, myself, will fly apart.

Phobias about words increase—chemotherapy, radiation, cancer, the doctors' names—I can neither say nor write any of them. I cringe when other people say the words, especially *chemo*, that common nickname for something so awesome and dangerous. Exhaustion mounts. Douglas and Khary decide I should not go by myself again, and they make up a schedule, taking turns accompanying me downtown on the days that Sally cannot come. When Adam is home, he comes with me. Their devotion strengthens me; my pride in my tall, powerful sons narrows the short period in the hospital with wide borders. The walk itself, even the subway ride, is an outing that fills me with joy.

On the last day of radiation, I choose to go by myself. On the way to the hospital is the huge open Farmer's Market in Union Square. Across several city blocks are rows and rows of colorful plants, country-bred flowers, every kind of fruit, vegetable, home-baked bread. I buy corn, plums, a lush plant called Wandering Jew, a large bunch of red, yellow, and pink zinnias for Jamar and Raisa, two dozen black-eyed Susans I recall my mother naming for me as we drove down a country road in her beige Dodge, her violet dress matched by a purple flower in her hair.

Now, the people I came in with six weeks before are mostly gone, and a new crop waits in the outer room. This small world filled with scary images and a sense of being a part of the doomed will go on, far beyond my treatments, and Jamar and Raisa will offer their kindness to others, some of whom, perhaps, will be as emotional as I have been. Meanwhile, my breast will heal, the darkness will fade, and even the scar will grow shallow, becoming more of a line than a gouge out of the flesh.

Before I leave for the last time, I call Jamar and Raisa into the room. I put my hands on their shoulders and tell them they are immensely gifted health care workers, that I could not have gotten through without their sympathy and support. "Coming from you that is really a compliment," Jamar says, and I feel that somehow, thanks to their unfailing respect, I have preserved some dignity. I embrace them both and walk out onto the street. My grief is enormous, shapeless. It leans on my chest as I try to breathe. It surrounds me with breathless emptiness. I will not be able to give it name or form until all the treatments are over, and I still have two chemotherapies to go. But I know I have come through something that has changed me forever. I walk a city mile back to the subway, weighted down to earth by the flowers and fruit in my arms.

There are many days during the months of radiation and chemotherapy when Lois comes to my apartment and remains all day. She understands the comfort of having someone in the house when you are not well and feeling weak, even if you have no specific need. She usually sits in the living room, watching television, doing her bills, reading, or napping. I lie in bed thinking of her childhood, growing up in poverty, shunted around from relative to relative, her mother dead when she was five, her father dead before she was born. I am trying to imagine her grief narrative, the words she might use if she had the confidence, the endurance, or the opportunity to write them down.

Above all, coldness undermines me, makes me feel culpable, faulted, ashamed, long before I feel any anger. Writing this, I am suddenly feverish, my skin goes hot, my face burns.

I feel the old grief of losing everything, so there must be some memory of union, or why would I feel loss and not emptiness? But I have no actual memory, only the image of my mother I saw in an old family film made by an uncle when I was a child. She is holding me on her lap, my long legs touching the ground. I am pouting and she is gently mocking me, poking my lips into a smile as she smiles at me. For a moment she is an ordinary mother, I am an ordinary child. And that is all. All the rest is fantasy or cruelty or an incessant, active nightmare that illuminates everything with its shining outlines of the deepest, thickest black.

I am sitting in Aaron's room. Every Friday, it seems,

there is a storm outside, a perfect reflection of the storms I feel within. He is looking at me intensely, and I feel the immense relief of someone listening. I talk on and on, then stop, embarrassed, and say, "I'm afraid you must be thinking, what in the world is this woman talking about?" He says, "I am thinking that, but not contemptuously. I am thinking, with interest, What is she talking about?" Not to judge, or condemn or even solve with earnest intention, he is just listening, perhaps closely enough to understand. In the strength and honesty of his emotion, I find my own. I think of Sally in the book-lined restaurant, of Anne and Irene walking with me up and down the San Francisco hills.

Before shame and anger there is simple need. Between unworthiness and desire lies a loneliness too large for form. Against such shapelessness, what chance is there for a small arm around a mother's neck, the graceful sloping curve of a breast? Only an image, a perfectly chosen word, a brief moment of intimacy itself.

Out of Her Mind

At times internal movement is too fast to keep track of easily. Like the blizzards of this past winter, when the sky turned white and everywhere showers of white fell onto white-covered streets, a solid blizzard of feeling storms me, blurring outlines with an indiscrete wash of pale gray. This is, in some ways, the hardest part of the story to tell, writing about writing, a story about loss of myself. It is spring now, but I remember the mountains of snow, six feet, ten feet, and higher, lining the sidewalks only a few months ago. At first a beautiful mixture of solidity and translucence, they soon become infested with garbage, opaque with street pollution, old papers, food, dog shit, like the piles of garbage my feelings of goodness can suddenly become.

A dream, several years old, but still haunting: Gloria is still alive. Although she knows she is going to die soon, she is serene, even joyous. In a lush garden, she plants and hoes, turns dirt over and under, preserving and packing roots. Nearby is a small bookcase stacked with papers and books that she gives to me. I look into it and realize the contents are mine as well as hers, and as I am leafing through them, the bookcase becomes a stream of clear water. Now, I am looking into the bluish green water, seeing my reflection and hers. She is wearing a red dress, its buttons opened to reveal her breasts; her hair, though in reality it was brown, is a beautiful shade of gold. I feel a familiar and paradoxical sense of tranquillity and excitement, the way I feel when I am in my deepest concentration while writing. I take the papers into a room in her cottage, place them on a table by the window, and gaze dreamily at a wide, peaceful lagoon surrounded by spring-blossomed trees. And then, suddenly, like a theatrical curtain falling, a steel door drops in front of the scene, blocking out my view. The door is old, stained with rusty paint, cracked and broken, covered with mold.

When I have this dream several years ago, the country is beginning to spin far to the right and many people are feeling out of control. Budgets by Republican administrations on all levels of government drain social services, ignore human needs for housing and health care, promise increasingly punitive measures for prisoners, even petty criminals, and for teenage mothers on welfare. Over the next years poverty will surely teem over the cities even more than it already does, colliding with the dangerous injustices and precarious securities of our lives; the suffering and violence in store for some of us seems almost unimaginable.

A disastrous personal aspect of this radical shift in American politics is that Douglas has been out of a job for months. Most of the places he might have found work in his lifelong career in progressive government are now controlled by Republicans of the most conservative bent. A large group of former government officials at all levels are competing for the few positions in the private sector that replicate the social, legal, and employment services these people are trained to manage and direct. Our future, everything we have worked for, is suddenly insecure.

As months go by and I witness the daily job search, I remember when I was a teenager, the years of my father's unemployment. He walked the streets for hours, he would tell us, ending up in a diner where he drank cups of coffee until it was late enough to come home. Eventually, he settled into a sorrow that never completely left him again. I think of a close friend, a successful businessman, who was out of a job for several scary months, how he told me he would walk around and around the park, eat in luncheonettes, sit and read in the library, afraid to go home to the silence of the telephone. I was afraid this disaster would break Douglas in some way, that he would have a heart attack and die. I thought of all the scholars I had met since entering the world of university teaching myself, people who are hired part-time so that institutions can save money on salaries and benefits, people who are regularly "excessed" or "let go," who are unable to do the work they love with any of the securities or dignity supposedly afforded to workers in this country; of all the accomplished artists who cannot do their work because there is no regular money to pay for it; of all the people who have no work at all. Work sustains us — work we are committed to, good at — work that is paid for and structures our days.

Douglas is philosophical, as always, and after some time he obtains several consulting jobs, which, in addition to my teaching job, keep us going, but I am frightened. Everything is precarious. Like many "middle-class" people, we have regular debt that must be paid monthly, nothing saved, and no family money to fall back on. I have known Douglas for thirty years, but now for the first time I comprehend the real meaning of his heroic optimism, how, growing up as a Black man under American apartheid — the virulent and diminishing form of racial segregation known as Jim Crow — he learned how to survive. No rejection or disappointment keeps him depressed for longer than a few hours. Every new possibility is met with enormous hope. I try to imagine his childhood from the many stories I have heard: an intensely curious child, always out of the house, gifted and smart, often secretive, but once involved, deeply committed, first to sports, then to school, eventually to love. Far more pessimistic by nature, I nevertheless try to follow his example, to keep my hopes up, to spend a certain portion of every day literally counting our blessings. I write them down: my children's achievements, my job, our health. But I am weakened by the griefs of Gloria's and Simeon's deaths and the losses their dying raked up in me; and by anxiety attacks I fear might never be overcome; and now I am frightened of losing the greatest sense of safety I have ever known.

I am kept going by demanding work, my book about race for which I have a good contract with a major publisher. The book began forming in my mind years before a word was put onto a page. It came to me first at a reading I attended by the German writer Christa Wolf whose essays and fiction have influenced my writing and teaching for many years. In my notes on the back of the program I wrote: "As writers, we are in love with formal beauty, the traditions and histories of word designs. Yet, we dare not rest in that simple ecstasy. There is too much evil in the world and it has been perpetuated by too many generations." Like Christa Wolf, I live in a country whose history centers on one of the greatest evils ever known: the enslavement of over fourteen generations of African people. My own ancestors were not implicated. They were poor and working-class Jews of Eastern Europe and came here only in my parents' generation. But my children, who are African American, still suffer the consequences of this holocaust. I decided that evening to write a memoir about my experience of living in a Black family for twenty-five years, raising Black sons to manhood, about how my entire consciousness and perspective has changed as a result of imagining American history and culture from a Black person's point of view.

After two years of writing outlines and notebooks and submitting proposals to publishers, encouraged by my agent who believed strongly in the project, I finally obtained a contract with a large New York house and an editor who was not only successful but on her way to becoming powerful in the industry. Indeed, while I was writing the book, she moved to another publisher where her position was even higher and more prestigious than before, and she took my book (then in its early stages) with her, a common sign of an editor's confidence in a work. She loved my proposal, and I allowed long-sobered hopes about being published responsibly and intelligently to rise dangerously high again. I reminded her repeatedly that this would not be a simple memoir, as was the fashion of the day, a story moving like a conventional film from scene to scene. Mine would be a book including various tones of voice, told not in linear time but shifting between present and past—for that is how I understand real psychological change to occur—and I wanted to replicate honestly an experience of deep transformation. I told her that I was interested in conveying what I had learned about white racism and that, although their voices would be heard in every chapter, my children's lives would not be the center of the book. I knew this focus on myself, a middle-aged white woman, was less sexy than the story of two young Black men coming of age in racist America, but the editor supported both me and the idea. Her excitement deepened mine.

Even at the earliest stages, I understood this book would serve many agendas for me.

I wanted to speak out against racism in the tradition of African American autobiography I study and teach, to think and feel my way toward a public and audible voice on this most critical American reality. I wanted to undo what Christa Wolf calls a "fabrication" so that contradictory feelings and new insights could emerge onto the page, but I knew I would risk criticism and disapproval, as there is no subject more fabricated in American life than race.

But the ordinary dismissive rejections any artist in this society experiences repeatedly, the pain of being ignored until aspiration comes to feel like grandiosity, self-respect like false pride, had caused a break in my confidence. I had begun to resist the periods of confusion and chaos in any creative work when images are disparate, ideas and feelings only vaguely sensed, irrelevant and all too relevant thoughts surfacing into the mind from some place beyond conscious control. My feelings of self-doubt increased until I reached a point in the draft where the shape emerged, connections came into focus, and I could begin to work within a sensible, perceivable design. Only that later stage of work could block out in me internalized voices of contemptuous critics trivializing women's autobiography, especially when the woman's voice is passionate and emotional, not offering optimistic assurances that everything will be all right.

Like most writers, I had taken great pleasure in learning to see formal intention in literature, which helped me gain control over the structures of my own work. But shadows of my childhood fears and desires, which I had tried to illuminate in my work with Gloria, darkened and grew. In some part of myself I began to subscribe to the dichotomy many of us create between emotional intensity and formal elegance, a dangerous opposition that can make honest expression impossible.

Through teaching, I tried to work out a compromise: If I could articulate a synthesis for my students, perhaps I could find a way out of my own dilemmas. In my nonfiction classes, I taught *Notes of a Native Son,* by James Baldwin; *In Search of Our Mothers' Gardens,* by Alice Walker; and other essays whose designs were elegant and accessible yet conveyed enormous passion. I tried to find words to impart this convergence I needed to see more clearly myself: that passion and order are not opposites. Indeed, in the strongest writing there is a dovetailing of structure and emotional revelation, and if you find the words to describe one, you will have a sudden glimpse into the other. In Baldwin's *Notes of a Native Son,* for instance, James, the son, can come to an understanding of his own story, his battle with rage and injustice, only as he begins to comprehend his father's story. Structurally, this classic and brilliant American essay uses a story-within-a-story design. The outer story, the death and funeral of the father, is the occasion for the inner story — the son's growing consciousness of his own rage against injustice, his passionate need to be seen for who he is. The outer story gives the inner story shape, and yet is unraveled by the inner story, itself changed.

In my fiction classes, I tried to help my students see the beauty of literary structures so they might bring more conscious formal attention to their own work. We built detailed outlines, learning to track the images that come into the mind unexpectedly, to use them with intention and purpose. We made maps.

At the same time, I was inspired by the easily exposed, raw emotional intensity of my writing students. They reminded me of a nearly lost self, of the way I wrote before I began to distrust my own passions. My feelings spilled over, of course, into panic attacks, bouts of shame, and explosions of rage. But the spillage became more and more rare. Twice I had an ulcer attack. I became too exhausted to write except in my journal, which I now thought of as permanently secret, not merely private; a record I would eventually destroy.

I hoped that the subject of my new book (a political and social issue I felt strongly about) and its form (the consciously reasoned personal essay) might serve as a bridge to some new capacity for unifying spontaneity and discipline, passion and control. I tried to prepare myself for periods of resistance and the anxiety caused by unclear first drafts. I reread the last work I had written purely from inspiration, with no notes or planning ahead. One night, I sat down at the kitchen table, filled with emotion about Adam's diabetes, and a perfectly organized story emerged. When I was finished, I felt exhausted and drained. I still liked the story, and I saw that the very process that had once enchanted and compelled me, the thing that turns people into artists in the first place, what is called inspiration, or talent, the part that comes before craft and before art, the deep, personal, mysterious need some people have to repeatedly, often ecstatically risk expression of the inner self—all this terrified me now, made me feel I was in danger of losing my mind.

Because of my insecurity, I was showing the editor, my agent, and her assistant each chapter as it was completed. When I felt embarrassed by this need for approval, I reminded myself of Virginia Woolf's words that it is no use telling writers not to mind what other people think, because writers are by nature people who mind very deeply what other people think. All three women responded with excitement and encouragement, said they felt emotionally moved and intellectually changed. The editor referred to revisions here and there but assured me she meant nothing dramatic. I became very dependent on their reactions, on their voices urging me to go on.

Although I was teaching full-time throughout most of the writing of the book, I was as disciplined as I had ever been in my life, sitting down at the computer or with my notebooks every single day, making my way through five long chapters. I gathered my stories about what I began to call "the whiteness of whiteness," a state of blindness I saw as the ignorance and denial of the impact of racism, both its history and everyday late-twentieth-century life. Extracted from my journals, then rewritten in notebooks, finally onto the pages of my narrative, I created a method for reworking the stories into a coherent draft. Once the anxiety of the initial draft was past, I relished the revision process, clarifying, shaping language and internal structure as I had for so many years insisted my students do. For those weeks of crafting, I was in control and felt I was regaining strength for the next period of uncertainty when perhaps I could dismantle the long-erected wall in myself—a steel wall that comes down suddenly, blocking my view of a beautiful lagoon, protecting my spirit from attack, but also imprisoning, shutting out my most personal vision of the world.

When I look back now, I am awed by how much was riding on that book for me. I was reworking my own past, writing for my children, but also for my parents. I remembered my mother teaching me how to draw a face, framing my childish pictures and hanging them on a special part of the living room wall, telling me I was an "artist," and for years I had understood the significance of this naming for me. But my art had become the art of words, and my father was a man of words whose lifelong activism and unswerving dedication to the fight for social justice I had always admired. I was writing my way through a kind of writing block, caused by deep disappointments with the reception of my previous books. Not least, the promise of a decent sum of money was due when the manuscript was complete.

As I retell this story now, I remember all that I have learned about the way any work, even a simple job well or poorly done, can reach into the bottom layers of self, bringing up old associations of dignity or shame, touching a bedrock sense of self-worth that moves and shifts dangerously in some of us. I know I have marveled at the solidity of that foundation in Douglas, in my own children, and recognized its precariousness in most of the writers I have ever known, including myself.

When I finished a complete draft, I gave the entire book to my readers, the three women who had been critics, muses, and friends.

And now the most banal part of the narrative, the familiar disappointment, or disaster, of a publishing experience that has happened to so many in the past twenty-five years as the industry has become subsumed in enormous multinational corporations, linked to the corporate film industry, dealing in million-dollar contracts and returns. Banal, even cliché; but damaging, nearly crippling. And should we not speak of this loss too, give it the respect, at least, of visibility, of being told in our own voices, the chance to be grieved without shame?

My editor was on a rung of the corporate ladder that was very near the top, and her business reputation must have been paramount to her at the time. Her immediate superior, the publisher of a large house, must have disliked my book, or failed to understand it, or even merely seen that it would never bring in the money books are expected to earn in these times. No one ever told me any of this. No one ever acknowledged a superior whose judgment killed my chance for an honest reading. I only assume it, because my editor reversed herself completely, deciding that she did not like the book after all, that it was unmoving, unclear, and not at all what they had expected, which was a linear narrative, a straightforward family memoir, the story of a white woman individually overcoming racism through understanding the pain (not as significantly, the strengths) of her Black family. She denied that I had described the form and subject to her from the beginning, that she had loved the book up until then, most of which she had already read.

Racist critiques were made with astonishing shamelessness. The various (unnamed, unseen) readers, my editor told me, wanted to know when in my childhood I had "fallen in love with black skin"; whether my sons were dating white or Black women; they felt my sons, who were college educated, presented as thoughtful and gentle people, somehow "did not come through as authentic young Black men."

Most damaging of all in a way, because here my own convictions were weakest, their sources still unconscious, I was told by the woman I had trusted and relied on for a year that my book was structurally chaotic and organizationally incoherent. When I tried to explain the shape and meaning to her, she implied that I was too defensive to take criticism, that I could not cope with the reality that my work needed to be thoroughly changed. After a three-hour meeting during which I only barely defended myself against these charges by stating firmly that I would not rewrite the book according to her new specifications and accused her of lying to me about her former opinions, I left the office in a daze that, by the time I entered my apartment, had become a full-blown rage, and in a week's time had transformed into one of the most overwhelming depressions I have ever known.

Later, when the book was submitted to other publishers, several white editors complained of being emotionally unaffected, that the narrative left them cold. During this time, I was encouraged by many trusted readers, some of them Black, and by the intense appreciation of a largely Black audience where I gave a reading. Eventually, when the book found a new publisher, I was told that the emotional effect was intense, that many readers even cried. Perhaps, the white editors who were "not affected" were unable to grasp stories about Black people, unless such stories center on the familiar and stereotypical signal of violent rage, or are written by those whose reputations for earning large sums of money for publishers are already assured. I was learning more than I'd bargained for about what it felt like to be Black, caught in the mazelike structures of racist history and racist institutions, the existence of which most whites are pleased to remain ignorant of for as long as they possibly can.

Yet even now I write against deeply ingrained cultural assumptions that we must take full personal blame for every failure, whether in family life, professional achievement, or the arts, that understanding the broader political contexts of our failures, or of our achievements for that matter, is only an excuse. The cream rises to the top. If you're good enough, and determined enough, you can make your dreams come true: a half-truth, crucial to remember when one is falling into self-pity or false blame; dangerous when the odds against you are more powerful than any single individual's capacity to defeat alone.

I dream I am working on the computer and suddenly all my work disappears. The screen presents, instead, a basic lesson in how to use WordPerfect, my word-processing program. Patterns I thought I'd overcome years before close in on me again, and I follow old narrow tracks with hideous ease. I begin to feel secretly crazy, convinced "I cannot read the world right," as I have named this feeling since I was a child and asked all the adults around me, "Is my mother going to die?" Then heard them say, "No, of course not, how could you say such a terrible thing?" The despair is so unrelenting, the sense of unworthiness never to be erased so fully returned, a feeling of failure in the world seemingly so final, that for the second time in my life I make the decision to give up writing entirely. Thus, I lose my last defense.

I try to emulate Douglas's relentless optimism, his ability to leap out of every disappointment into renewed, energetic hope, but I am afraid we are both in danger of losing heart. We watch hours and hours of television, trying to relax and escape, becoming resident experts on every detail of the O.J. Simpson case. We talk of O.J. Simpson in the dark before we fall asleep, go over the hours of commentary on talk shows every night, checking off all the points that argue for his innocence.

Long after the not guilty verdict, when I am still in treatment for breast cancer and trying to unravel all the stories I am writing here, I will dream I am walking through a world of dark, underground caves. In one cave I see Simpson sitting on a rock, bereft and alone. He may have been found not guilty of murder, but he has been found guilty of being a bad person, so he must remain underground and in prison for the rest of his life. He looks into my eyes, and I see we are the same.

Ice mountains solidify, collect garbage until the garbage becomes the mountain itself. The steel door, even with its ugly rust and corroded paint, is the only escape.

I begin to take a sleeping pill each night, craving unconsciousness. For the first time in my life I have to remind myself to write in my journal. With the relief of the deep sleep provided by the pill, even dreams disappear. The moment I leave my classroom, or turn off the television, depression sweeps over me. I am invisible. I am silent. This downward turning feels life threatening, as if I am actually descending into a world of underground caves. It grows darker and colder. I am awakened in the night by intense sweats accompanied by the certainty that I have cancer. I am brokenhearted and fear a heart attack. My grief consolidates. I am enclosed.

During this period, the early spring of his senior year at Brown University, Khary and his friends at school, all of whom are Black, although from a variety of ethnic backgrounds, are increasingly harassed by the police. They are stopped on the street without reason and asked for identification, even threatened. Their parties are broken up violently, false accusations made about selling drugs and liquor. One of Khary's close friends is arrested and taken to jail, where he will remain frightened and angry all night. Khary and another friend jump into a car to follow him to the station house, determined to be witnesses and thus lessen the chances of police brutality. But as soon as they start the engine, they are surrounded by several police cars screeching to cut them off, "like in some cop movie," he tells me. "I have the right to see what happens to my friend," Khary says to the encircling police, and one cop, his hand on his gun, shouts, "You have whatever rights I say you have."

Every day, Douglas and I call deans, assistant deans for "minority affairs," the head of the college police who himself was once a member of the Providence force. He speaks with careful respect of "African American young men," assures me he knows it is natural for college students to have loud parties and question authority, admits that when Black young men are having parties and questioning authority, police immediately tend to suspect they are part of the drug world. He acknowledges the accuracy of the reputation of the Providence police for racism and brutality, "worse than in L.A." "But I told them," he says, "that Khary and his friends are good guys, and not to even think about harming any of them." His need to say this escalates my fear of what might happen on any given night when some young African American college student, possibly my son, decides to question the authority of a cop. Then he tells me he knows just how I feel because his own son, a member of the Providence police force, has been targeted by a local gang for death. Silently, I wonder whether the young man has been brutal or unjust to provoke this targeting. Nevertheless, I sympathize with the father, terrified for his son's life. As parents we feel the same, although our sons are on opposite sides of what Khary has called a war. But this is the man who was Khary's primary adversary on a university committee formed to address the question of college police being armed. He wanted his men to carry guns. Khary and his friends wondered how many Black students would be shot "by mistake." Several hundred miles down the East Coast, I am wary and desperate. I beg him to keep an eye out for my child, to negotiate with the police. Nothing is sensible or controllable. I am unable to protect my son, and white society at all levels denies the racism threaded into every social structure, every individual mind. At some point, with college intervention, the crisis lessens, but it does not disappear. The police have labeled the house of Khary and his friends a "trouble spot." At the least, they are robbed of the pleasures of late parties during the end of senior year. At worst, they may be in real danger. I count the days until graduation, realizing the stories I've collected in my book will never be done. I begin to fear, as Derrick Bell and others have said, that American racism is permanent, incurable, an evil we shall never overcome.

I enter into a period in which my journal is obsessed with fear, self-doubt, and self-deprecation in relation to everyone and everything. More than a year later, these pages are still painful to read. The desire to contribute to public conversations on issues about which I care deeply and have spent my life exploring—motherhood, race, the uses of autobiography to reflect on history—feels doomed.

There are two equally important aspects of a writing life. One is the bedrock temperamental need to continually, as Adrienne Rich put it in one poem, "turn one's life into words." The other, which grows as one ages, is the need for impact, for recognition, and thus contribution. Can a woman of fifty who has been writing for twenty-five years have the first without the second? And if not, what possible replacement can there be? These questions plague me and seem unanswerable during the winter and early spring following the shock of this rejection. When I walk from the subway to work, or from home to the store, I have the desire to lie down on the pavement and just go to sleep. *She is out of her mind,* I hear someone say as he passes my body in the street. I stop for a moment, staring down, strongly attracted by the possibility of not taking another step.

Toward the end of April, after a year of searching, Douglas finally gets an interesting and apparently permanent job. Two weeks later, I go for a sonogram to test a hardness in my right breast, which I am certain is just the cystic breast tissue I have experienced in the past. But as soon as the radiologist touches me, I see recognition in her eyes, and the needle biopsy she gives me then and there confirms I have breast cancer; a discrete lump, she thinks, hopefully easily removed, she reassures me, but nevertheless a lump. Cancer. A disease that mystifies doctors and researchers with its power to return. In that sense, incurable, at least in any definitive terms.

And in that moment, standing on the street with Douglas, both of us in a kind of shock, my depression lifts. As if by a harsh, swift wind, despair is blown away. I notice it immediately—the heaviness gone. I am terrified, but also energized by a kind of gathering determination I can only call hope.

Reaching back into a past I thought was all but lost to me, I begin to write obsessively. I write about my feelings, record information, take notes on the medical knowledge I have to master in a few days in order to make intelligent decisions. I write in hospital waiting areas, on examination tables waiting for doctors to come into the room, on subways, at home whenever I am not occupied with something else. Long-obscured feelings are suddenly stark and clear. Now I can name the deep and dangerous shift I felt: a loss of faith, or belief in the spirit of my life, as if it were over, nothing to live for; what one writer I read long ago called "a leftover life to live."

At first, I am writing only to maintain a sense of control. But slowly, after the surgery is over and the period of treatments begins, words assume their old magic again. I am intrigued by their heft and weight, entranced by their music, their capacity to represent so closely what I feel inside and notice in the world. I dream the old dream of finding an unused, dusty but spacious room behind a door in my apartment, a room I had forgotten was there.

But I feel a stranger in my body with all its aches and pains, its weaknesses and inabilities, its threats. I lean on everyone, can't lift a box of groceries, get through a day without sleeping, or a night without crying. It feels insufficient to say, simply, that I am afraid I am my mother and therefore dying despite positive medical prognoses; or that many people feel illness, especially cancer, as a mysterious, personal failure, resistant to ordinary comprehension and controls. I can list all my griefs, but I can't knit them together. I need some more specific center. I need to see, or create, a structure in order to understand.

When my younger sister Emily comes from California to stay for several weeks, and accompanies me to the first, most frightening, chemotherapy, I look at the woman and remember the little girl. I held her in my arms as we clung to each other in our beds, nights increasing into years as our mother lay dying in her room through the kitchen and down the hall. I remember feeling enraged, wanting it to be over, wanting them to turn the lights on in that room. But those thoughts quickly sank into darkness, and habitual insomnia began. After our mother died, I would crawl into Emily's bed, pretending I was there to protect her, letting her fall asleep on my shoulder as we listened to our father pacing and weeping outside our door. I remember her long blond hair, which I envied and adored, the intense blue eyes that marked her, and not me, as our father's child, the small, thin body I smacked in anger, leaving long red marks on her fair skin. I remember reaching out for her hand as our family cruelly divided us, she, her father's child, I, my mother's, each of us deprived of half a sense of belonging, which in different ways became not belonging anywhere at all. Over and over, I remember staring up at them as they narrated their divisive mythologies and reaching down for my sister's hand.

Emily is a painter and sculptor, and during one long period she painted double portraits. From each canvas, two faces looked out at me, the two earliest, most familiar faces of my life. Both cast as women, one had my father's features, and one my mother's. But the woman with her features in certain paintings could also look like me, and in another light I could see both my sister and myself in my father's face. When she is sitting in the living room after the chemotherapy is over and I am lying on the couch, nauseated but relieved, I feel an enveloping comfort. When she touches my arm, I feel I am safe at home.

It is always difficult to call a new therapist, to ask a complete stranger to listen to the most detailed narratives of one's most personal life. But with Emily's encouragement, I call someone recommended by a friend. I was surprised that I was calling a man, and told myself the defining reason was that his office was within walking distance of my apartment. Now I realize there were old and reliable securities embedded in his maleness, a belief in survival itself. When I first meet Aaron, I am struck by his kindness. I have no hopes or anticipation of the profound changes I am about to undergo.

During most of the summer, I swing between strength and weakness, confidence and fear. Then, one night, I awaken from a nightmare in a rage so intense I am screaming. Incoherent sounds, roars, or cries are coming from my throat and I cannot stop them until Douglas shakes me. I know I have dreamed about my former editor, the woman who betrayed my book. Like a child changing a monster into some ordinary, familiar shape, I have to turn on the light to wipe out the image of her face in the dark.

I describe this experience to Aaron, and we spend the hour sharing feelings of anger at the lies that made me sickened and sick. After the rage is out, there is space inside that slowly fills with unconnected memories. Over the next few weeks, I carefully avoid planning what stories I will tell to begin my session. I do not search for insights to bring him. I do not want to present myself, but rather to speak about whatever comes to me at the moment, to feel the relief of getting it all out of my mind. *Out of her mind*, I think happily, enjoying the echo. And now I see that the accusation of structural chaos was key for me, and I recall old memories, forgotten for years.

My mother's slender, elegant body is covered in the long pink bathrobe she wears after her morning shower and her evening bath. Her feet are clad in high-heeled slippers, stripes of silver and blue. It must be the morning when she is getting ready to go to work, because I am choosing a flower from the artificial flower drawer, then a folded handkerchief from the neatly stacked pile in the handkerchief drawer. I am changing the contents of the brown bag to the blue one to go with the blue suit with the black velvet collar and cuffs. I have no idea if my mother would have imposed her love of order on her daughters. Perhaps she was a freer spirit, comfortable with or even fulfilled by a child's difference from herself. But after her death, her orderliness and elegance were idealized. As a teenager, I preferred dirty sneakers, torn black sweaters, and tangled hair. As a child, I threw tantrums and toys around my room.

I am a small child, sitting in the middle of a messy room. I am surrounded by every toy and piece of clothing I own, a sea of chaotic possessions, playing first with one thing, then another. My mother is sitting on the bed screaming to someone else that she cannot control me, doesn't know what to do with me. An ordinary experience of many mothers and children, no doubt; but for me every moment of conflict with my mother, every passing anger, is attached to the memory of her death and my guilty sorrow, until over the years that central memory thickens, as if with layers of once-transparent glass streaked with grime, finally becoming opaque enough to hide the infinite variety of my badness. I am sitting on the floor surrounded by the mess I have made. My elegant mother is weeping, she is covering her face with her hands.

When I leave Aaron's office, I feel lighter, unburdened. In recapturing an old source of shame, which now feels like some kind of innocence, the newer sorrow diminishes. As I walk home, I have another memory. I am the mother now. First Adam, then Khary is sitting in a completely disordered room, and I sit on the floor, my back resting against the wall. I watch as my child begins creating a block structure in one corner, using everything on the floor as part of the construction—the blocks, other stray toys, pieces of clothing, a glass half full of juice, colored candies trailing dust from the pocket of his jeans, even a few old hardened crusts of bread from lunch. Out of this mixture of shiny, expensive toys and debris, a spectacular and weird structure is emerging. Blocks of various shapes lie sturdily atop one another. The glass of juice has become a glittering column holding up some sort of terrace upon which small wooden people walk and sit in tiny chairs. An orange Life Saver placed at the pinnacle catches the afternoon light. The memory is sharp and bright, my son so fully concentrated saliva is dripping from the corner of his mouth (when it is Adam), his tongue protruding through his lips (when it is Khary), as he creates a corner of balance and beauty, sitting amidst the disorder of his room.

As I walk down the street, a frigid wind snaps across my forehead. I lift my face to it and let it sting my eyes so that the tears from the cold can increase the tears already on my cheeks. In this image, I have begun to understand and thus recover the essence of my writing life.

During the afternoon following the sixth of eight chemotherapy treatments, I am lying in bed, hiding behind my telephone machine, as usual, unable to tolerate speaking to anyone for several hours after I come home. But for some reason on this day when the phone rings I pick it up. It is my former editor who is calling to congratulate me on reselling my book, cheerfully wishing me the best of luck. There is a long moment of stunned silence. I feel a clean, hard anger move up into my throat. In a tone of furious warning I tell her never to dare call me again, that I do not know how she has the nerve to contact me, that if she wants to convey any message, she should do so through my agent, and I hang up. For the next twenty hours, I am violently ill. I vomit every ten minutes or so, throwing up everything in my system, and then, when there is nothing left, gagging on my own bile as if the entire world makes me sick. I will never know if this extreme reaction is the result of the juxtaposition of chemotherapy with four weeks of radiation, which the doctors suggest is possible, or if it is related to the phone call, the sound of her voice denying the impact of her actions, my regurgitated rage replacing the self-effacing and muted response I controlled myself into having in her office six months before.

For the next few months I begin to plan this narrative as if it may save my life. I will weave my story with fervent yet skeptical faith that somehow, if I get close enough to the least-apparent truth, I will complete my cure. Not only must I write my narrative to strengthen that mysterious entity, my immune system, but by the time I reach the final pages, I hope to glimpse some bedrock reality about my experience of these successive griefs that suggests a bridge to walk on from here. I want a structure that is stone solid, yet flexible, so that I can accommodate alterations I discover along the way. An outline of sorts. A map.

While I am still in the middle of treatments, I receive a call from an old friend, my former stepmother, Maurine. She came into my life when I was twelve, like one of those old unknown rooms in the back of a house that suddenly sheds a different light on everything that was there before. She is a profoundly optimistic soul, involved with lifelong spiritual and physical disciplines of all kinds, an actress and director who, though she never gained a wide reputation, has grown more and more serious and accomplished through the years. She is in her middle eighties now, and she is calling to tell me she has recently been diagnosed with breast cancer. Like me, she will be all right, a survivor, and in many of its particulars her cancer is similar to mine. This experience frees something inside me. In that extra room, sheets are suddenly swept off old furniture, the furniture itself moved around to frame a clearer, more open space. If Maurine has breast cancer, though its source may include an insidious combination of physical and spiritual weakness, there is one thing it is not. It is not punishment. For who would punish so sunny and sturdy a spirit as hers?

And so I know, in a way of knowing far more certain than mere analysis, that I am not being punished. Not with cancer, not with any loss from death or coldness or some ever-present ordinary or extraordinary risk to my children's lives. In that moment of relief when I see loss and pain and even maternal anxiety as life's sorrow, and not a purposeful infliction aimed at my own guilt, I see its opposite more clearly than ever before. All my griefs, disappointments, and conflicts have felt like punishments to me. Punishments not only destined, but deserved. "You are not guilty. You must stop looking for your badness everywhere. You didn't kill your mother. It's time to leave it go," Aaron nearly shouted at the end of one session when I had equivocated, always stopping short of exonerating that little girl waiting for her mother's death, never exonerating the woman for any mistake, limitation, wrong word, any failure to provide. And I begin to wonder if the weight of his insistence might be strong enough to undermine the lifelong cast, an acquittal to prevail against a prison so long lived in it feels like home.

My stories have crowded his room, and I am opened as I do not recall being opened ever before, as if a sharp scalpel has slit apart my mind like a sharp scalpel slit apart my right breast. My oldest rage and griefs had flowed back into my system, flooded it with poison, breaking down immunities built up over years, immunities I thought were reliable, protective, learned. But there was a fault in the structure. Broken down like a dam attacked by a hurricane, the structure cracks and breaks and the story pours through.

Inside, there has always been a channel, or what I have called a channel. Suddenly, it opens and I am in a place where the deepest connections I see easily find language. This is what I have been resisting, rushing to fill the hectic space with ordinary tasks, company, reading, television, anything to dim its stunning intensity.

Writing these pages, nearly a year after my surgery, I

am amazed at the truth of that sentence. I was afraid I had nothing. As if I didn't have my children, Douglas, the other people I love; as if I didn't have the Wellfleet Bay on a cloudy day, its tall grasses and soft waters; the exciting combination of deep red and gold, or the tranquillity of pale green near a grayish blue; as if I didn't have the perfect words, *a sense of unworthiness never to be erased* or *intimacy itself*. I was afraid I had nothing. My vision cut off by a wall of steel, there was nothing to keep me from death.

This is the climax then, the moment of creation, the transformation of the layers and sources of my feelings into some alternative form, a corner of careful building to place them out of my mind. I am aroused. As with the emphatic, rhythmic percussion of an orgasm giving both ecstasy and relief, my body is alive with liquid sensation. I cannot, like some, plan and order my dreams, but I descend to the hard ground of my channel and I kneel down. There is my spirit, or heart, washed out of the cave by a storm. It lies on the damp sand, beating.

Remake

If I were able I'd say it. Say make me, remake me. You are
free to do it and I am free to let you because look, look. Look
where your hands are. Now.

—Toni Morrison, *Jazz*

It has been five months since the last chemotherapy treatment. During this time I have lived in a state of near
solitude and inward focus bordered only by the comfort
and security of Douglas and Khary coming home each
night. Even then, they are both quiet souls. We share
news of the day, eat a meal together, and then, often, I
return to this room, this chair, where I pull out my notebooks and narrative and descend again. At times I feel
guilty for this long period of self-involvement. With no
students to teach, no children to raise, little connection
to much outside my own mind and imagination, there
is no daily giving to ground a sense of goodness in myself. Self-preoccupied, even self-absorbed, I am regularly
accosted by critical voices reminding me of all the extraordinary troubles in the world and ordinary needs of
family and friends. But I have had a kind of vision, a seeing into things I cannot ignore. I will return to the world,
I tell myself, the needs of the people I love, work with,
share life with. But surgery, chemotherapy, and radiation
did not complete my cure. I am certain of this. I have
interior jungles to journey through. I dream them all
winter, darkened thick places where narrow paths twist
ahead of me in unmistakable invitation. Cars and trucks
are leaving just as I get to the stopping place in the road.
I am waiting at desolate snow-filled stations for trains
that are so late I fear they may never come at all. Suit-

cases filled with old possessions of my father's and my mother's are locked in storage while I try to find the claim ticket that will prove they are mine. Often, I am carrying a small child in my arms—a blond baby, or an olive-skinned boy—who has been in my dreams for as long as I can remember. It is apparent I have to walk each step of this journey burdened by no impediment to my energy for looking within. Only the most personal writing enables me to feel secure, to wait on the roads and stations with some sense of faith that I will reach a destination, a place to lay my head.

Children are so sturdy. They can make survival accommodations to wounds and losses and cruelties and injuries with seemingly endless variety. But we are also fragile creatures, for in those accommodations we amputate and cripple parts of ourselves. How did I finally get to this place after so long a time, to be able to retrieve my mother's photograph from the bottom of a hutch drawer, frame it, and hang it on the wall? How did I come to be able to wear her pearls, which I've had almost all my life and have never been able to wear? Somewhere in my notes, the clear line of the story must be evident, and I want to follow it now. This time chronology serves, for it is the end of the narrative of my grief.

It is December, a few days before Christmas. I have recently completed the six months of treatments for breast cancer, and slowly my energy has begun to return. One evening, I am waiting for members of my family to arrive from other cities. I am cooking several dishes for dinner, stopping to clean out rooms and empty dresser drawers for guests. While I work, I am listening to choral music, and behind the voices a rhythmic beat of a bass keeps track. The repetition of song and beat builds sensuously until I am high, gaining and losing myself in the same moment of joyful energy. This is how it begins. A feeling of life, my brain finely tuned, my body pulsating with passions of all kinds. I believe I can find the words for this narrative, that I will be free of disease, and behind it all, the image of Aaron's attention during my sessions, his memory for detail, his interest, the intensity of his gaze.

I remember having this feeling many years ago after a cervical cancer scare, which was resolved with minor treatments. I remember living in its sometimes blinding glare during the year I became, and then passed, my mother's death age of thirty-eight. I thought I could have and do everything. My power was limitless. I felt I could change the world. Was it then I became certain, as well, that every failure or loss was a punishment of the magic girl I shamefully believed myself to be?

Like a dry canyon slowly moistening and filling with water, my sexual feeling intensifies, sometimes just a general sense of sexual life, not directed at anyone in particular, spread out and medicinal, as though old cells are being healthfully rearranged. Throughout January, the strange happiness continues, strange because it is wedded to an explicit articulation of grief. I write out the details of my recent sorrows, relive the treatments I have only just escaped, trying to sort one thing from another or gather what seems similar into one place.

The beggar girl I thought I'd locked away has returned with all her greedy hopes and hopeful needs. I touch her filthy rags. I run my fingers through her greasy hair. I look her in the eye. I have always known the roots of all my fears lay in childish terrors, but now I feel the connections as if they were my own pulse or breath, see them as clearly as blood drawn from my vein. My anxiety is triggered by a certain kind of anger. I am impotent, then terrified. I am the victim and the furious attacker. A child is pounding her fists against a slab of stone. As the weeks go by and I am increasingly focused on describing her, my anxieties begin to diminish, not to dissolve, but to lessen considerably so that I am able to keep them under control before they rise into panic. Now, if Adam doesn't call, I imagine he is busy, not in danger or ill. If Khary or Douglas is late coming home and sirens screech down my block announcing multiple disasters, I watch my fears begin, but I am more often able to remain calm. Sometimes I truly believe they are unharmed. When I see the beggar girl is not me, I glimpse the possibility of safety and well-being. When I see she is me, I find her sad and beautiful, a desperate, harmless child.

I buy myself a new Walkman and begin to listen to Mozart's Clarinet Quintet in A, then become especially compelled by the second movement. Because of the earphones, the music seems to be inside my head, within my own imagination. As soon as the clarinet solo begins, joined later by the violins, then the clarinet again, a low cello behind, I am forced downward, as if hypnotized. I am literally entranced. For a moment it seems possible that the meaning I sense will burst into language. I suddenly feel my breaths going deeper, taking longer. I feel my blood slow down.

As the winter proceeds, I spend more and more time with the dead. My memory is crowded with scenes, old voices, old dreams as vivid as the ones I had the night before. One night, listening to the Clarinet Quintet as I write, I remember how much my father loved music. I see him pacing back and forth in the living room, humming and weeping, as a Tchaikovsky piano concerto plays over and over on the old record player. I open a box that contains a few of his belongings: a Timex with a broken black band, a pipe, a pair of blue woolen gloves. I was leaving

his apartment and heading uptown. It was a cold afternoon and I had no gloves, so he took his off his hands
and gave them to me. "It's cold," he said, "put on some
gloves." I wore them home, and several days later we
found him dead in his room. He was a gentle soul, full of
love and anxieties: perhaps because of his childhood in
Russia, always threatened by local Christian anti-Semites
and their pogroms, as well as by his father's brutal beat-
ings of his brothers, his mother, and himself; perhaps because of his life as an American Communist, imprisoned
in his youth, for years followed by the FBI; perhaps because of the loss of a young wife whom he loved deeply,
leaving him with two young daughters, one of whom he
found difficult to understand. He used to tap each piece
of furniture ritualistically each night before he went to
bed. After a turbulent marriage to Maurine and a painful divorce, he was increasingly and intentionally alone.
Toward the end of his life, when he was sixty-seven, he
fell in love for the first time in years with a woman much
younger than himself, but she, like my mother, got cancer and died. Soon afterward, he had a heart attack, and
two years later he died. But when I was a child he was a
charismatic and magnetic man. I remember his passionate laughter and anger, his lectures to me about American
fiction and Marxist theory, the approval that sometimes
shone in his pale blue eyes. My love of words originates
in his voice commenting and arguing, his ongoing analysis of politics and love. Even now, I converse with him in
my head. I miss him with all the longing of this difficult
year. But my father died when I was twenty-eight. It is
my mother I know I have to find.

One afternoon, six or seven past journals spread around
me, my narrative in progress open on my lap, writing first
in one place, then in another, I realize that the essence of

radiation was loneliness, and that loneliness has always been at the heart of my life. Yet even loneliness is a recovered feeling, and every recovery feels precious. I cling to it for days, suffering and brave. I feel another sea change, as Gloria once described that long-ago transformation. Tides shift dramatically. Sea life from far-off shores is suddenly rampant and close by. The very feel of the water is changed. At times I feel crazy, thinking about my daily obsessive, joyful, sorrowful digging. I feel slightly mad. By now I am listening to the Quintet many times a day. The music is exquisitely familiar. The relationship between the violin and the clarinet in the second movement brings Aaron's face into my consciousness almost as visibly as if he were sitting in my room or I were still in his. I conjure him up. My feelings for him are a towrope. He fishes me out of dark water where the ocean meets the bay. In that dream he is a sea monster who looks like a tall skeleton. A *see*-monster who rises from the dead, surprisingly benign. Gender differences melt back into narrow, distant margins. In the center, I feel a sense of protection. I feel loved. During the sessions I am aware of a familiar yet odd luminosity to his skin, although when I enter and leave the office he is an ordinary man.

In February, Gloria has been dead four years. I reread her obituary, several of her articles, stare at her photograph. Aaron tells me a story about a little girl he once knew, his daughter's friend. She had been through a traumatic experience in a hospital, a severe illness during which time she had to be separated from her mother and her home. Afterward, she would visit his family and play with a dollhouse, but in her play the dollhouse would always be a hospital, the dolls nurses, doctors, and patients.

On a plane heading for the West Coast, I am writing

in my journal as usual, listening to the music. Perhaps it is because I am on a trip by myself for the first time since being ill, or because I am literally above the earth, suspended in the sky, but suddenly I emerge from what has become this ordinary state of extraordinary intensity. With great pleasure, I watch a light, foolish movie about love, which also pretends America is really a good country; a Clinton-like president setting it on the right track by telling everyone what values really are; how we really do know right from wrong; that as a people we must take care of others or lose care ourselves. After watching the movie, I begin to rub a smooth new vitamin E cream into my hands. These two small, effortless activities are the kinds of thing I could not do as a child and young woman without paralyzing self-consciousness. Ordinary tasks seemed to belong to a universe from which I was excluded. Others might be lighthearted, pleasurably superficial. I had to be vigilant, keeping track of the dead. There was a time when I couldn't dress without great anxiety but, instead, had to throw on one particular black sweater over one particular black skirt and rush away from the mirror as if in escape. I noted the easy sensuousness other women had with their bodies, their homes, but all that seemed precluded to me. I was always afraid I would lose all memory of what I was supposed to do if I didn't keep still, sit and stare, write everything down. I rub the cool cream into my hands and remember the time in my life when I could not do simple things, but always had to be that little girl, making a hospital out of a dollhouse.

As the weeks go by, the harmonies and rhythms of Mozart become part of my consciousness, connected like a keyboard to the strings of my concentration. Each time the violin reaches for its highest note and the clarinet responds, the music suggests a place of belonging—within —and a way to get there—writing. On March 1, my mother has been dead for forty-six years. From a high shelf I take down the few possessions I retain of hers: a handkerchief, a string of pearls. Touching them, I am in a long moment of ecstasy. I feel a sense of being open and the desire to be seen, to be known. I hear my children's voices, *Watch me, Mommy, watch me.* And I watch, the boy running faster than ever before, the child swimming his first strokes, the infant lying on his back and gazing up at my face as my hands caress and attend, his legs pushing at air, his arms flailing, his whole body moving with excitement and pleasure.

Several weeks later, a late March evening, the world outside my window is dark. I have loved the early winter nights and am sorry to see the days becoming longer. The night makes me feel more alone, as if the world I have been living in is an actual place outside me. The dead, the ungrieved losses, the banished feelings metamorphose around me into visible, tangible shapes. They surround a woman who stands alone in a courtyard, and I know it is the courtyard behind the arches in the painting on Aaron's wall. The woman is singing, talking, repeating sounds I cannot translate into words but whose meaning I know as surely as I know there is music in my ears, darkness in the outside world. The work of the grief narrative is to recover the original desire of wanting my mother more than life but terrified of death, which is where she is. I must recover this desire so its hopelessness can be separated from all other desires, its horrible futility leaving me with shame or with dread or with nothing or with rage. I remember her in bed in the hospital, in bed in her room, sitting up and laughing in the afternoon, lying in the dark, sitting in a wheelchair by the Christmas tree, taking a cinder out of my eye as I stand on the closed toilet under the light. She is emerging from the bathtub before she pulls her pink bathrobe around her. She is placing a Kotex between her thighs.

I write the details as they come to me and then the shading between her and my children blurs. Boundary lines between bodies and passionate loves evaporate, and the blending is so brilliant it is like looking into the sun, I fear my eyes will burn, that I will lose my eyes. The clarinet plays what the strings played before, a long phrase whose beauty I thought was gone, and I am in a split second of time when I felt adored the way I adore my children, their flesh, their faces, their skin magical, luminous, absolutely singular, irreplaceable. Then their eyes are on my face and I am irreplaceable, absolutely singular, illuminated and adored. Aaron's words from nearly a year before, "You are not her, but you are her daughter," gain substance, shadow, a rich tome of subtext and implication. "I call her Tullah. I never call her Mother," my cold answer, months later. I have known a narrow pit of loneliness, a place where no one could ever find me again. Now, I move slowly into the shadow of her being, this time not obliterated or insubstantiated, but a mother's daughter like all the other daughters, not in some weird sense motherless, a being who can never belong.

I remember nearly a year before, my surgeon leaning over me, undoing the surgical stitches from my breast. With tiny scissors she cuts each loop then pulls the slender, colorless thread out of my flesh. A neat scar remains, but for several months afterward I am afraid the incision will open like a seam coming undone and expose my wounded tissue leaking blood.

Now I feel the same, too open for the world, nearly

faint walking down Broadway. Yet, I am solid in a way, strong enough to face this new, eloquent pain.

For weeks, each time I turn on the music and the strings begin, I hear the sound of my own voice narrating stories of old love, anger, and gaping need. In the echoing clarinet, I hear Aaron's voice repeating my words to me in a different tone. She is emerging from the bathtub. I see her body clearly. Her thighs are like mine, her breasts smaller like my sister's, her face is composed, not yet decomposed, short black hair sleek from the water, cut close around her head, skin olive smooth. She pulls a towel back and forth across her back. I see the graceful slope of her waist, the tiny indented valleys on either side of the base of her spine. She puts on a sanitary belt and attaches a Kotex to both ends. Does she stroke my face? I don't know if I am remembering or imagining but I see her stroke my face, smile slightly, and while this image is in my head another image joins it, as if one picture is superimposed on the other yet both can be seen at the same time. I am sitting in Aaron's room. He is watching me closely, his attention so focused and powerful I can relax for a moment, for an hour, I can trust it will not disappear.

The words *my darling* come back to me, and I remember when she died, thinking, Daddy calls me Baby, or Sweetheart, or Ketseleh, I will never hear darling again. Now I begin to hear darling in my head whenever I encounter a person, or image long beloved. When I see one of my sons. When I hear the phrase at the center of the second movement of the Mozart Clarinet Quintet. When I see Douglas's face in the gray darkness just before I fall asleep. Even in lines of poetry that seem to name perfectly some inchoate feeling of my own. *Hands dripping with wet earth / head full of shocking dreams.* I see the movie *Jane Eyre,* a novel I have studied and taught and loved for many years, the story of a motherless daughter written by a motherless daughter in which both writer and character take possession of the narrative of their lives. The actress is so like my image of Jane it is as if she is Jane, and when I see her face on the screen for the first time, I think — my darling — as if I have found someone lost long ago. But I do not say the words out loud. I keep them to myself, a private sign of other emotions suddenly possible to share.

I take the pearls out of an old box. A block away from my house is a small jeweler's, an old-fashioned shop run by an old man who can fix anything. I show him the broken clasp, but it is nothing unusual, no big problem for him. He only needs to know if I want gold, or silver like the old one. I want silver, and in two more days I can pick it up. "Good pearls," he tells me, "worth fixing." The first time I wear them is in April when we go to Los Angeles to see Adam in a play.

As I sit in the audience waiting for the play to begin, fingering the pearls, a memory comes to me. In his first year of college, his first time living away from home, Adam's adjustment is made infinitely more difficult by the onset of diabetes just after his high school graduation. He is vulnerable, though as always excited to be out in the world. One night he calls me after seeing an old movie about a mother who is banished from her daughter's life. He describes the plot, the mother poor and unloved, watching her daughter's marriage into a wealthy family through a crack in the doorway of the church. Then, as her daughter emerges in a flowing elaborate gown, she edges in from the back of the crowd and tries to identify herself, but when her daughter sees her she turns her head from the shabby stranger. He is crying as he tells me the story, and I keep asking, but why are you crying so much? "I don't know," he repeats. Then finally, "I just know I have always been haunted by your mother."

I have often wondered why this generally sturdy, sometimes fiercely bounded, confident son was so fragile in the face of that story of a banished mother. Now I think perhaps he took in my anguish and my anger. A child with an almost frightening receptivity, perhaps he was unhinged by the conflicting emotions this empathy gave rise to in himself.

For hours after the play, he seems distracted, recovering from the powerful emotions that are written into his part. As I watch him exchange the intensity of art for the restraints of ordinary life, I see him as a strong, separate adult, my child elusive, and all weekend my eyes burn with tears. Yet the emotions he brings to the part come from his life story, which branches out of mine. There in the man is my boy, my child, my infant, the heavy turning mass inside my body, the solid flesh and skull pushing down the river of blood and pain between my thighs. I have begun to recover my mother through memories of my children's childhood. Their small hands on my face. Their dark eyes staring at me as if to penetrate my skin. Then at last, after nearly a year of incomprehensible cries and generic gurgles, their voices, and in the memory of their voices finding a name for me for the first time, I hear the faint sound of my own child's voice calling the lost name.

A picture forms in my mind and spreads out, forcing everything else into the shadows. I am looking down at my mother in a coffin, as if the coffin is on the floor and

I am standing over it, looking inside. But not only did I never see my mother in a coffin, coffins are not generally placed on the floor so that a child would be standing over it, looking down. Then the image changes suddenly. I am high up, in my father's arms. I am looking down on my mother in a hospital bed. I am about to leave for my aunt's house and must have sensed I was seeing my mother for the last time, so I have asked to say good-bye. The room is dim. Her face is tiny, skeletal. Thin brown arms lie across pearly white sheets. And I say softly, because I have been told over and over to speak softly in this room, Good-bye Mommy. She doesn't answer. Her eyes are closed. There is no response.

Once again I am uncertain if this is actual memory or imagination, a scene generated out of the formless energy of emotion. The relation between fiction and autobiography has often been a problem for me, and I am always making up scenes. But I know I retained a lifelong discomfort with a certain kind of silence. When I speak and no one answers, I am filled with anxiety, then anger, then desperate need, then hopeless, grief-stricken love. And that is what I am sure I remember as my memory or fantasy floods my consciousness, what I buried all those years. How much I loved her. And so I realize I love her now.

I remember emerging from anesthesia and the feeling of Khary's hand in mine. His large palm, the sharp knuckles, his oddly small nails. Willing to do anything to penetrate the fog and see his face. Gripping his fingers. Hearing his voice. Climbing out of lost time.

In our hallway is a black hutch that once belonged to my great aunt, my grandmother's sister. On a low shelf are albums of photographs carefully organized by time and place. But in three drawers, the overflow gathers into a thick, disorderly pile. Baby pictures of my children, my nieces and nephews, lie right on top of Douglas or me as infants ourselves. I am a young woman with long brown hair, and an aging woman whose hair is white. My father is holding Adam, the only grandchild he lived to see, and he is a young boy in the old country, his facial structure and features remarkably like my nephew's, my sister's son. At the very bottom of one of the drawers is the old portrait of my mother that once was framed in green leather and stood on our bookcase when I was a child. She is wearing a scarf with the triangular point coming over her forehead. Her smile is broad and passionate, her dark eyes full of life. She suffered a terrible illness, died young, and was then exiled by the stories that spun around her corpse, buried in old boxes and the bottoms of drawers. The injustice of it catches in my throat. I frame her picture in narrow gold, like many of the other old family photographs I have hanging on a wall. It will be necessary to take some down, move them closer together to make space for hers, and I do. I take some down and move them closer together to make space for hers.

And now I don't want the reiteration of all the blame and anger, not now, not when I've finally remembered her thighs, her breasts, the color of her skin. I don't want those old harangues, complaints, confessions, rage attacks, that guilt-ridden self-defense, not when I walk by the wall and see her face at last. After all these years, I am able to pull a towel back and forth across my back when I emerge from the shower without it feeling like a dance of death, back and forth until I'm sucking her earth, unable to breathe, trapped down there before my time. No.

Those screams of don't leave me, and anguished waits for her returns, those vague and numerous losses that still leave their precise tracks, all those are for some other time, future or past. But not now, not in this moment when I turn the necklace around so I can see what I'm doing in the mirror and slip the sharp point into the tiny filigreed box. The clasp is just like the old one. The pearls fall gracefully across my bones.

And what is left to describe? In recent weeks, I have been x-rayed, mammogrified, the inner lining of my uterus biopsied, my blood tested for every kind of disease including cancer. I am fortunate, a survivor, and for now the story of illness comes to an end. I would never say I am glad I had cancer, yet it was cancer and my stories about it that cured me of an even more obscure and enigmatic affliction. I no longer feel the dull pain of amputation. Somehow, as if miraculously, I no longer feel masked.

It is nearly summer again, and I will revisit the ocean, Sally's peaceful house, the Wellfleet Bay. There are no more tests scheduled until September, so I will assume, each day with a joyous sense of peace, that my body is healed, its scars clear but fading. My breast is permanently darkened, it seems, the area beneath the scar sensitive to pressure of any kind. It feels as if everything inside is in pieces, just like wood or some other solid mass might feel if burnt to a crisp, broken apart into cinders and coal. I hold it at night, stroke it, remembering the dark silhouette in the radiation machine. I have been told my mother had a double mastectomy when they were still trying to save her life. I do not remember seeing that terrible injury. I do not remember feeling her breast against my cheek. Perhaps if I began with these images, however, I might be able to reconstruct that story. Language is the carrier of passion for me, its absence the sign of irretrievable loss. It is also the labor that gets me through my days.

The work of recollecting memories is not over, but everything can never fit into one story. Rather, I must choose the elements of each piece of work. A crucial time in my childhood that changed my life forever, the memory of which might change my life again. This strange and unique love for a therapist who listens so closely he enters into the inside of my stories while still remaining separate, different from the rest, staring at me from an ordinary chair. A piece of music I become enthralled by, listening to it until it is the background of all the feeling rising up within me, then the foreground, the subject that contains all the others, the very thing itself.

The violin begins, the clarinet echoes, then the two melodies separate into harmonic difference, an erotic and sorrowful relation, moving over each other, away from each other, back together again. It is the brief moment when the two instruments overlap their notes that draws me down to a place where I have only tears, then out to a desire for words. I have listened over and over trying to get at what it is about the overlap that thrills me each time, and all I have come up with is this: the low note is held by one, the high note of the other enters into precisely the same moment, and in an ecstatic comprehensible instant, all my grief and love is transformed into melody.

As I write this sentence, I write memory instead of melody. Your eyes on me. Your voice responding to my voice. Surgical threads stitched, unstitched, then stitched again. I find no perfect chords to bring this story to a close. But when I put on my earphones and listen, I encounter an alluring shadow of previous intensity. Then I am back in the revelatory darkness within a series of arches. I look around and feel *my darling*. Someone is listening. The earth beneath my nails is damp with blood.

And now when I reread my own words and once again come to the closing pages of this narrative, I see that even the pattern I have followed here might shift again. In a sense it is arbitrary where I bring this story to a close. Gloria was right. When I am in the midst of a book it is as if my mother is back with me, and when the work is done I have to let her go again. I have only recently remembered that in an unpublished novel I wrote when I was just past being a girl myself, I imagined a girl visiting a beautiful enclosed park on cold afternoons. In this park — was it bordered by arches? — she would see her dead mother, who could not speak or be spoken to. But she could be looked at, and she could look back in return.

Memories come to me in pictures, vivid scenes or vague impressions. But I find the pictures are elusive unless I preserve them with words.

It is Sunday night, our regular "book talk," and my father's questions are about the book we have both read that very week. Beneath us is a worn green rug, to my left, floor-to-ceiling shelves stacked with books. The black desk where my mother stored her beautiful accessories is his desk now. Scattered papers cover a torn green blotter for his fountain pen. Reflected light from the windows across the street jumps and slides across the large window at the end of the room. My mother has been dead for about three, perhaps five years. My younger sister is asleep. My own bedtime, an hour later in honor of my age, is as far off in time as the end of a journey when a journey begins. My father's white hair waves thickly back from his pale forehead, around his unusually large ears. His blue eyes behind large glasses have always conveyed a sense of mystery for me. Different from my dark eyes, from my mother's dark eyes, his are overwhelming somehow, like the sky. In his large rough hands, he holds the Russian novel he has assigned that week. He spreads the navy blue covers, opens to a page marked by a navy blue satin ribbon attached to the binding, and begins to read a passage aloud. He may pause to tell me a story of his own childhood or youth in the early years of twentieth-century Russia, stories that, because he is an emotional man, often evoke his laughter or his tears.

Light in golden streaks shines from the yellow shaded lamp whose copper base is glistening, dark orange, golden brown, crisscrossing and complicating the light already on the window pane, and I think I do not hear my father's words, I am so enchanted by his laugh, and laugh in response, then agonized by his tears and I cry. But when he asks me for my thoughts about the book, I somehow have been listening after all, and he seems to like the words I find to answer him. When my words are right and my father admires them, I forget for a moment that my sister's blond and blue-eyed beauty is easier in his heart, that I don't have him all to myself, that my mother is never coming back again. I will never forget this feeling, repeated in classrooms where I am a student, then a teacher, in intimate conversations with friends and lovers, in therapy sessions, in audiences when I read from my books, the knowledge that the other person likes my words. Nor will I ever forget the opposite, when I know my words are failing somehow, graceless, disharmonious, horribly flat.

At times, sitting in my father's room with its dark greens, pale blues, and copper light, I feel mute, in some kind of swoon that is both erotic and dangerous. What is inside me that I might let out now? What must I hold in, sitting on my heel for hours until my face turns red and my father sees what I am doing and shouts at me to go to the bathroom. But he cannot force me, of course. I hold in what I must. Over the years, I try to comprehend what I might shape well enough to release.

Once you have had breast cancer, the chance of having it again is greater than before. These are the statistics, numbers which are one sort of language to describe history, no less real than loneliness, itself the trail of loss too great to be mended or restored. But I have survived cancer twice, once my mother's, once my own. Both times a charged, powerful desire for life infused me, the first time searing guilt into the thick fabric of my loss, the second time forcing me to narrate old stories once again.

This time I don't want to forget anything. Not even the nightmares, or the shock of possibly impending death. Once again, I am walking through the doors to the operating room, lying down on the table under an enormous light. *What are the names of the books you have written?* Later, I am holding Khary's hand, frightened of lost time. My right arm must have been placed at an odd angle because for several weeks it was sore, its muscles aching differently from the pains caused by the loss of lymph nodes. My doctor must have needed the arm to be raised and pulled to the side so she could cut a neat line, peel open flesh while someone blotted blood, looked for the signs.

Nearly two years later, my arm will still begin to ache like an old sorrow suddenly real again in one of those too vivid dreams. I lay it against the softest pillow of the three I use, the one in the silkaline pillowcase, delicate white embroidery bordering its side. I do not really need such luxurious comfort now, the ache is dull, the sharp pain beneath the scar on my breast occasional. But I want to remember the nights when the pain was so bad I wept, so I can remember the nights I cried in terror that I was going to die, so I can remember how certain I was I wanted to live as long as I could, and what was important and what was not.

Sometimes lately, I sit still and silent in Aaron's room and try to bear a feeling of liquidity, of slow, out of control, undulating movement. I am more comfortable now with interior confusion, with stories not yet formed, desires not yet protected by a crafted phrase. Time moves but does not always tick its seconds so audibly, with such extraordinary threat, and even when I am not writing, I can occasionally forget its relentless movement, allow its velocity to slow or quicken in response to the quality of a moment, the recognition of some simple or enormous need. I look around at the small, carved animals Aaron collects — oak, rosewood, ebony, some of them streaked with silver lines — lined up on a high bookcase, standing in a circle on two low shelves of glass. When I look at the animals, I think of pain and desire, their inescapable impact, their natural brilliance. I think of the preciousness of ordinary life and of the strange, hard truth that outside fiction, some stories never end.

Jane Lazarre is on the faculty of Eugene Lang College, New School for Social Research. Her books include *Beyond the Whiteness of Whiteness: Memoir of a White Mother of Black Sons*, and *The Mother Knot*, both memoirs published by Duke University Press; the novels *Some Kind of Innocence, The Powers of Charlotte*, and *Worlds Beyond My Control;* and a volume of essays, *On Loving Men*.

Library of Congress Cataloging-in-Publication Data

Lazarre, Jane.

Wet earth and dreams : a narrative of grief and recovery /
Jane Lazarre.

p.   cm.

I S B N 0-8223-2206-4 (cloth : alk. paper)

1. Lazarre, Jane — Health.   2. Breast — Cancer — Patients — United
States — Biography.   I. Title.

RC280.B8L298   1998

362.1'9699449'0092 — dc21

[B]   98-10116